Series "Illustrated fairy tales for adults"

◆◆◆

The Adventures of Percival

a phylogenetic tale

◆◆◆

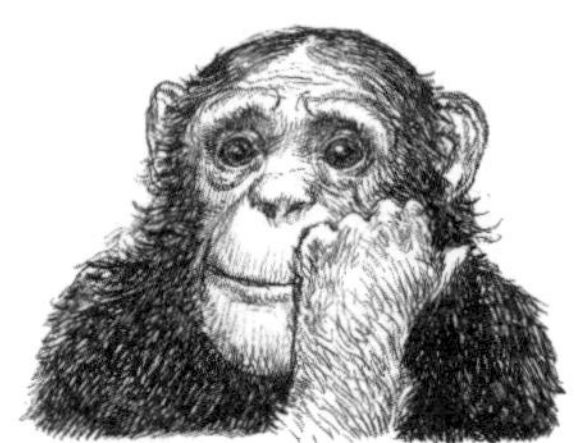

PRODUCTION TEAM

Pierre Senges: writer

Nicolas de Crécy: illustrator

Dominique Lestel: philosopher-ethologist

Alain Richert: landscaper-botanist

Paul Buck & Catherine Petit: translators

Lili Fleury: graphic designer

From a proposition by

Danièle Rivière: editor

THE ADVENTURES OF PERCIVAL

A PHYLOGENETIC TALE

by Pierre Senges

illustrated par Nicolas de Crécy

Prologue

As the famous axiom says: *Once upon a time.*

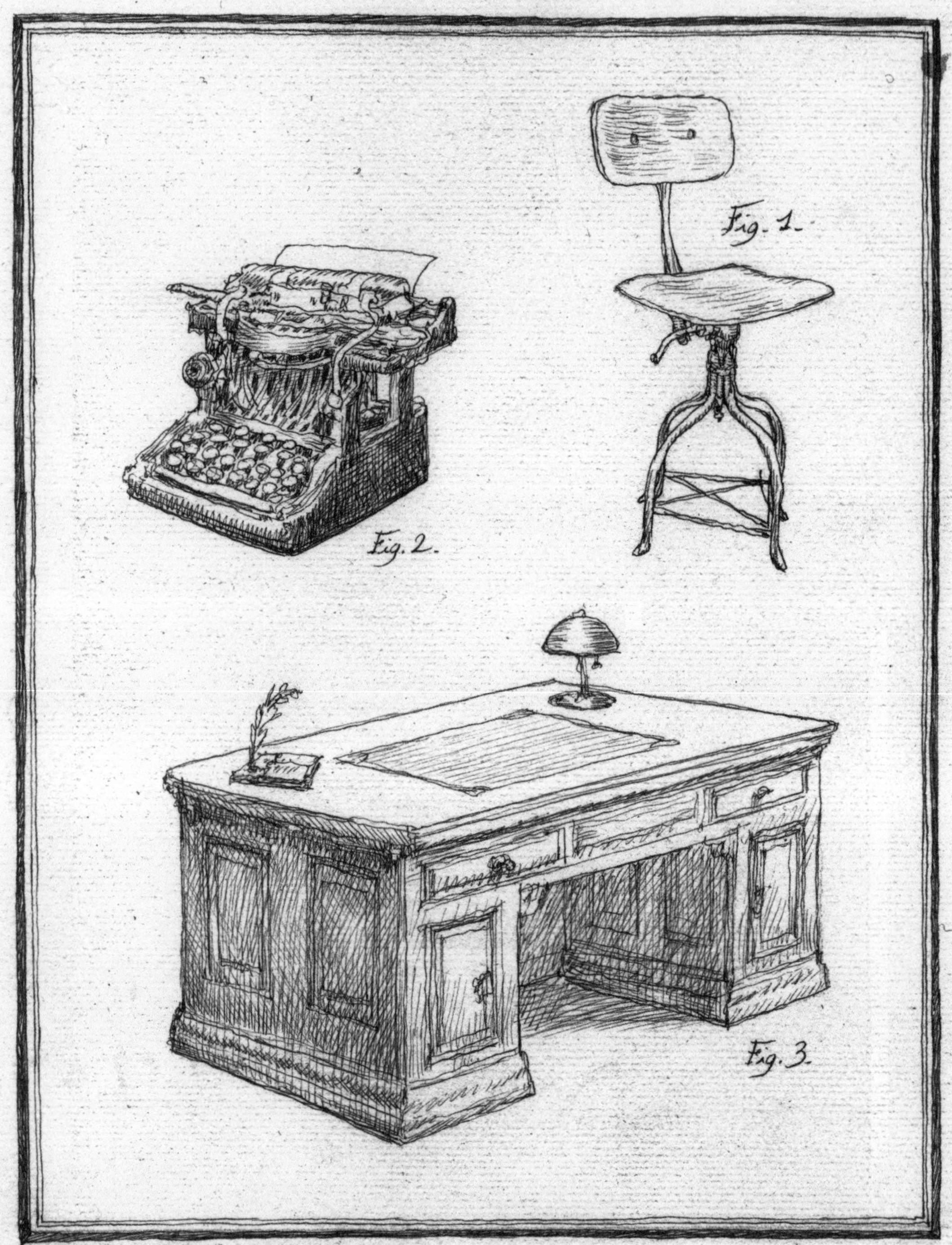
Fig. 1.
Fig. 2.
Fig. 3.

Chapter 1

THE ANIMAL ENTERS THE STAGE

How to narrate our story? To go back to a formula already enunciated elsewhere, in other circumstances and about other subjects: *several versions of the same fable exist* – some clear, some obscure, some loopy or bombastic, or spicy, ribald, austere, lewd, suave or rhymed in alexandrines; and some, so far from the original, benefiting from a new freedom by combining the alphabets, that one can only find one single authentic word, one only, or else three dots – and, to cap it all, in the wrong place.

As it concerns an experimental protocol, let's simply imagine a table and a chair: on the table, a typewriter, the ancient mechanism of a Remington (or Underwood or Olympia); on the chair, a primate: a chimpanzee, pan-troglodyte to be more precise, called Percival.

Chapter 2

THE ANIMAL STANDS UP

Genealogy of Percival the ape: his ancestor was called Sultan, the father of the line, a male of twenty-two kilos suffering from three boils, but without ever complaining (which distinguishes him from Karl Marx): in 1925 (nobody is getting any younger), in the laboratories of Wolfgang Köhler (*The Mentality of Apes*) he was that clever chimpanzee capable (for the first time before everyone else) of making use of a stool to grab a banana (one has to bear in mind that some scientists did spend their whole life hanging bananas from the ceiling). The jumping up and down of a chimpanzee on a stool stretching towards the sublime arch of a banana looks like nothing on an October morning in 1925, while Chamberlain is signing the Locarno Pact, but for all the chimpanzees, and Percival's family in particular, one should consider that as some sort of first step towards the attainment of an articulated reason. Eleven years later, in a world that had barely recovered from financial crisis (1936), Sultan's niece accompanied by her brother, supervised by J.B. Wolf, learns, in less than seven days, to provide food for herself with the help of rather ingenious tools (to have an idea, one should recall the key used to open tins of sardines): it was so moving, it was stunningly precise, and in reality the gestures of brother and sister have remained as effective as the day J.B. Wolf replaced the food (always the same old banana, always) with tokens (they could be exchanged for an orange or an apple — hard to know if Wolf was still busy studying the apes' intelligence or their aptitude to adapt to a monetary system, abstract to the point of villainy).

In 1951, during the Cold War years, Vicki, the pet chimp of the Hayes family *(The Ape in our house)*, the great-great (etc) niece of J.B. Wolf's pupils, showed herself capable of pronouncing the words *papa, mama, cup* and *up*, obviously in the awkward fashion that suits so well the female monkeys from the Barnum circus – so much intelligence, it has to be said, was coming from the bottom of her heart. 1969 was a year without equal, the year of the glory of glories (like 1955 for Maria Callas or 1963 for Jerry Lewis): a year that made fear fall from an incomparable peak: somewhere in North America, at the house of Beatrix and Alan Gardner, an eight month-old chimpanzee, eternally famous under the name Washoe, succeeded in mastering 150 words in sign language. One doesn't run the risk of making a mistake when one declares that never, until then (and very rarely since), has a chimpanzee from Sultan's lineage (thirteenth generation) been so close to Poetry (with a capital P).

In 1973, the triplets Bandit, Belle and Bido, Washoe's offsprings (from a second bed), perched on the shoulders of Emil Menzel Jr., demonstrated their extraordinary mastery of geometry; five years later, Sherman and Austin, Belle's sons, handled lexigrams under the watchful eyes of Sue Savage-Rumbaugh, D.M. McDonald, Rose Sevcik, William D. Hopkins and Elizabeth Rupert, which is a helluva lot of witnesses. The same year, Sarah, daughter of Bandit, in the company of G. Woodruff, David Premack and K. Kennel, obtained 88% of the correct answers in a test about the choice between the signs for *same* and *different*. She appeared to be only half-heartedly interested in the intelligence tests, though they were very exciting colourful devices similar to fortune wheels or the dials of our old phones (a handful of cashew nuts or a dry sardine as reward): one can see her most often turned towards the window rather than towards her game of detachable letters: yet, we see Sarah's talent blossoming, Sarah from the Sultan's family, the day she succeeded in associating the qualifiers *round, red* and *having a stalk* with the substantive *apple* – an exploit that today still many among our young prose writers seem incapable of matching (or even of wanting to accomplish).

In 1979, the fourteen month-old chimpanzee Nim Chimski, at Herbert Terrace and Laura-Ann Petitto's place, perpetuated the tradition of the uncle Washoe by learning sign language (each in his turn), though without displaying too much enthusiasm. In 1982, at Arnhem Zoo, in Holland, with Franz de Waal in charge, Mama, a very old female, a cousin of Belle and Bido, displayed before her death (the death of a matriarch, as they appear in Faulkner's novels: nothing breathes any longer, the rocking chair still rocks) the signs of her great wisdom.

Not so long ago Bemsha, Percival's grandmother, a lively female ape still in her youth, coquettish, a biting wit, suffering from the occasional crisis of melancholy, then cheerful again, a soprano coloratura who didn't give a fig for harmony, neither did she care for old Africa, Bemsha, goaded by Sarah Boysen and G.B. Berntson made a success of the until now unthinkable feat of recognising Arabic numbers and using them in the right way. Finally, the last great triumph of Sultan's lineage went back to 1986: it also marked the passage from elementary deeds to more glowing victories (one can see here the irruption of the laboratory's guinea pig at the heart of a quarrel between scientists): the day Alcofribas, Bemsha's son, combining two elements, having between them (I quote) *a semantic relation similar to that of the English syntax,* managed to paraphrase in a clearer style, smoother even, more convincing, the theory of a linguist from Massachusetts according to which the finite number of terms generates the infinity of sentences.

Sultan begat Pacha.
Pacha begat Semiramis.
Semiramis begat Ludwig, who had green eyes.
Ludwig begat Bemsha who re-invented the tooth-pick.
Bemsha begat Alcofribas.
Alcofribas begat Percival.

Chapter 3

THE ANIMAL WALKS ON TWO LEGS, THEN SITS CROSS-LEGGED

That's it for Percival the chimpanzee and his genealogy (we'll get to know him better as we go along: read about his adventures, observe his behaviour, understand his personality and fathom the depths of his soul, and that all done with great enthusiasm) – as for McIntosh, his breeder, his master, his friend, his lab assistant and his owner, the various versions of the fable present him sometimes as a mathematician by trade as well as an amateur gardener, and other times as a professional gardener and a weekend mathematician; in both cases, an occasional ethnologist: by conviction, through love for menageries and the animal kingdom, scrutinizing the chimpanzees for want of being able to climb trees still.

By the way, how old precisely is that Mr. McIntosh? According to some versions, he has his youth ahead of him, baby skin and candour – but according to many others, judging by his ivory-coloured teeth, and his gums and the white spots scattered up to his cranium where they become a little more lunar (if scriptural, in a way), judging too by his long fingers turned brown from decades of American tobacco use, one could give him seventy, *at least* seventy years, as if it was the Legion of Honour, and he was made the Chevalier of Gardens and Plants – and if that's not enough, eighty, to reach the birthdays of those venerable virtuoso concert pianists still at Pleyel to celebrate their eightieth birthday and laugh as they display dentures as precious as the ivory keys – and if not, ninety, to come closer to the biblical ages, hundred to round it up and emphasize the miracle; two hundred to leave the realistic world, that of the senior citizens pass and hypertrophied prostates, and join, through a keyhole, a cabbage, a rose or a mirror, the universe of fantastic tales.

How many times did McIntosh die and come back to life to have that air at the same time of being several hundred years old and being a naughty young man, an apprentice who makes blunders instead of learning how to live? McIntosh's resurrections are worthy of those of Munchausen, better than Rocambole (that one gets away with it through the backdoor and the not always miraculous tricks of the serial), better than Lazarus, of course, who seemed to come back from collapsing like a sack of potatoes to offer the witnesses a head shaped like a King Edwards. McIntosh, like Munchausen, skips instead of exhuming himself: his resurrections are twists and turns, like those which make two gossips, good friends, pass from one topic to another (according to other versions of the fable, the resurrections are a game with words: a fraud made with a biro, on a register, a date erased, re-written, a sprinkling of sand to soak up the ink: immortality for oneself and papers in order).

It has to be admitted: McIntosh, as he introduced himself, with his first name as Samuel or Stanley (depending), carried with him the tradition of four or five centuries, without showing fatigue nor pining for death – death like an eternal hammock stretched between here and the priceless afar.

Rather sympathetic: he boasts of cracking coconuts with a blow of one hand, of distinguishing between the fly (*musca domestica*) and the fly (*drosophile*) from twenty paces; about being able to make the lady's slipper grow and blossom on poor ground, on ballast, and even on a slate roof; about knowing the monkey as well as the monkey's banana, and being able to enumerate the genes that both have in common, by way of family likeness. He would have drawn the plans for the gardens of Marie-Thérèse of Austria, if he had lived a bit earlier, for those of François Joseph the First, and also of Maximilian, before offering his talents, the points of his shears to the modern republics, that of France and the Jules, that of Germany, that of Italy and numerous others, conflicting but fraternal in Eastern Europe (there he would have solved some agricultural enigmas in order to reduce famines: how to gather wheat without sowing any grain?). He would have travelled from Borneo to the Tierra del Fuego to collect other orchids, or some lichen, to study closely in order to understand their last mysteries; he would have lived with great apes, experienced the friendship of the last orang-utans, observed nests, collected termites and offered to the United Kingdom the culture of lianas, not for trade, but only for fun. He would have studied the path of a mushroom from the depths of a labyrinth, and measured the time taken to reach the exit; he would have cured the melancholy of an ant-eater from Guyana by reconstructing its biotope, flower by flower, to the smallest petal, for the love of the ant-eater and for the love of a job well done (according to other versions, it was an iguana).

One can see him sometimes dragging a bucket, walking in Wellington boots far too big for him, his legs two reeds in two vases made of rubber; he goes from one shrub to the next; he retrieves enough dung from the lions' cage to manure a patch of alfalfa: it requires true courage, the audacity of Munchausen, the audacity of Samuel McIntosh.

He is a man of practise and theory: according to him, any abstraction deserves to take its place in our superb (cumbersome, staggering, overwhelming) here-and-there: if only to entertain us and, after having amused us, give to the world extra reality forms. (Should we believe him, he would have offered to the soprano Elisabeth Schwarzkopf, as (her ninetieth) birthday present, a basket with two cats, "exactly similar",

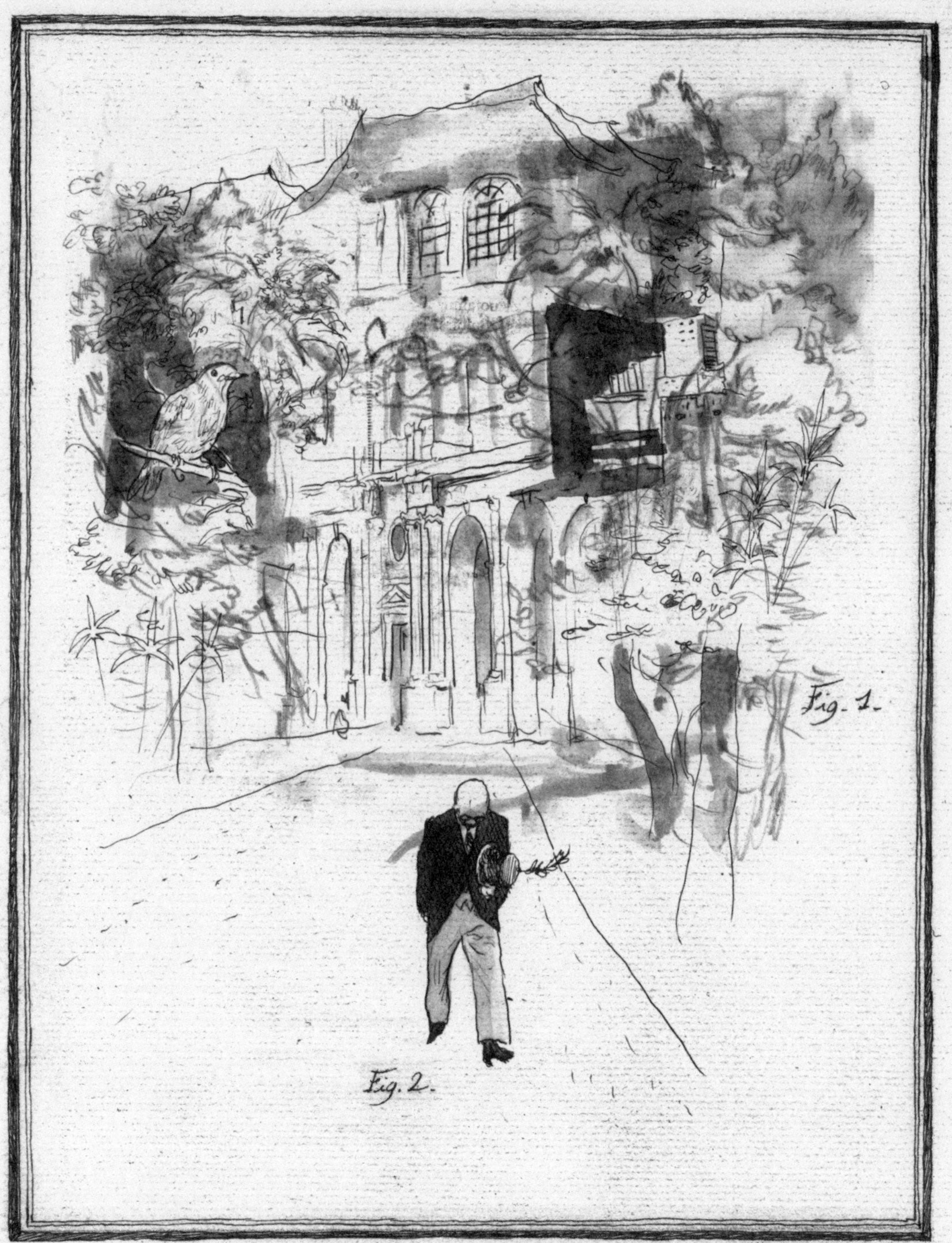
Fig. 1.
Fig. 2.

same beige and reddish-brown, same Abyssinian race, like two drops of milk, more similar even than twins, for it was two occurrences of the same cat. McIntosh pretended having perfected Schrödinger's machine, a not so simple mechanism made of a hammer hitting a phial capable of making co-exist next to each other the dead cat and the same living cat, in the basket; it was worth seeing, it was very touching (I was told), a little gloomy perhaps, but hypnotic: one of the two cats mewing the death of the other. After having squinted for a while, asked several questions, turned the basket upside down, called the vet, poured out some tears, confided all to her impresario and forgotten that sordid business of the dead cat, Elisabeth went to join another audience, covered in flowers.)

One gets to know about it from a reliable source: each Sunday, around midday, McIntosh gathers enough hot water in a tub to bathe himself: not out of concern for hygiene, there are showers for that: but out of concern for knowledge, to give Archimedes' theory, concerning the displacement and volume of a crown, a concrete application: he experiences that famous upward thrust equal to the volume of water displaced, then yawns, then rubs his eyes, then draws his conclusions, then soaps himself, one not hindering the other.

Chapter 4

THE ANIMAL REMAINS SEATED CROSS-LEGGED

Samuel McIntosh: imagine him tall, slender, capable of wide and high strides (remarkable strides), his arms accompanying the movement of his legs, and on top of all that, a hat, for as long as the weather is suited — and on the hat, a feather (let's extrapolate), like the tip of a seismograph. For the one who knows Munchausen, the tirelessness of the old man still alive past a hundred (a hundred years old cleared on the pole vault), his profile of elegant old nobility, vindictive and stubborn, his catalogue of lies (some containing other lies and opening onto legends), his audacity as an adventurer and sprightly beau, his total scientific curiosity, his appetite for knowledge, his appetite for trying to know, his even bigger appetite for setting up experiments, erecting circus tents serving as laboratories for physics and chemistry to embellish the world with colourful indicators, catalysts and precious precipitates, whose reflections are neither green nor blue — who knows Baron Munchausen will have an idea of Samuel McIntosh, doctor in Probabilities and Animal Behaviour. (The diploma — on his initiative and invention, drawn by hand, his own hand, and signed by him with the double title of rector and recipient — made him hope for the most exciting careers.)

To be a doctor is not always lucrative: some specialists of the gluon (which is a boson, of the group *boson of gauge*) have been seen becoming taxi drivers while waiting for better days to be carried forward to the next year — doctor in Probability and Animal Behaviour, Samuel

McIntosh has not found the door giving directly onto a corridor leading to an amphitheatre where he could have shone, like a lecturer. He has become a gardener, has found a straw hat, a pair of gloves, and a taste for that meticulous business: he has learned to take a cutting from papyrus, to cross two orchids to make one, to differentiate between oak and oak, to recognise with closed eyes the *Rafflesia arnoldii*, and even to cultivate apples (in other words, to cook them – especially that variety of apple discovered by one of his ancestors, a Scot who resettled in Ontario). Proud, at his age, to be in charge of a bit of land in the zoological gardens, his small plot, remote but thriving, luxuriant even, and peaceful, for nobody ever goes there any longer, neither visitors, nor the administrator, nor the personnel in charge of maintenance: the grass grows, the banana skin too, the remains of a hot dog in its wrapping, dust, dead leaves and some varieties of plums. He lives in peace and quiet there, in a rich desert (a desert dominated by philodendrons), he can feel like a king in here – in reality, far from the lions' cage and the office of the director, McIntosh hustles and bustles about as he fancies: roses, hollyhocks, water lilies or tomato plants (Crimean black variety). A map of the zoo on a scale of 1/500 would allow us to draw a line around his territory, almost two hectares of uncultivated land all to himself, a few unoccupied buildings, and an old elm tree that has become rare, with its wide and cracked trunk – McIntosh can take shelter there three days in a row (not in the elm, in his territory) without anybody noticing: he is not whistled at, he is not obliged to punch the clock and he receives his wage whatever happens.

Chapter 5

THE ANIMAL SCRATCHES HIS HEAD WITH HIS RIGHT HAND

The first visible version of the fable goes back to the year 1202, when Leonardo da Pisa had his *Liber Abbaci* published (before that it was nothing but a criss-crossing of legends and speculations, observing a very ancient custom). In his *Liber Abbaci*, Leonardo imagined three capuchin monkeys (*Cebus capucinus capucinus*): they are purely hypothetical, they gather together pieces drawn from an ABC, but pass away one after another before being able to put the letters of the proverb *Abbondanza genera fastidio* in the right order.

Half a century later Raymond Lulle took up the story again without quoting his sources, content with replacing the capuchins with three macaques (*Macaca fuscata*).

Around 1592, François Viète, a scholar at the court of Henry the Fourth, a promoter of the *logistica speciosa*, succeeded in reawakening those monkeys after years of sleep: they have become capuchins, of the white face variety, locked for seven whole years in a lawyer's office gathering together the letters of Marguerite de Navarre's *The Heptameron*.

In 1676, it was Leibniz's turn to take up the legend: the monkeys are reduced to one single chimpanzee, an ideal chimpanzee manipulating a rather ingenious device of rods and concentric disks until he obtains the first verses of the Bible, in Luther's translation.

The day before his death, which occurred on the 31st May 1832, Evariste Gallois outlined in the margin of a notebook a new version of the fable (incomplete) in which a chimpanzee called Gustave was about to write, without being entirely successful, the first seven verses of *La Carmagnole*.

It became necessary to wait for 1899 and Georg Cantor's version to finally see the typist chimpanzee provided with a typewriter and a comfortable seat; in 1900, David Hilbert urged that same animal, exactly the same one, to compose the complete first act of *Love's Labour's Lost* (by sheer chance).

In 1913, with Emile Borel (*Statistical Mechanics and Irreversibility*), the chimpanzees numbering a million, were placed under the direction of illiterate foremen (perfectly foremen, perfectly illiterate): one year is enough for them to compose an "exact copy of all the books of every nature and language kept in the world's richest libraries".

In 1927, Sir Arthur Stanley Eddington postulated an army of monkeys busy gathering on paper the entire collection of books held in the British Museum (*The Nature of the Physical World*).

In 1930, Sir James Jeans, quoting Thomas Henry Huxley, evoked six monkeys, not one less, and once again the library of the British Museum (or one single sonnet by Shakespeare, which is not bad at all).

John Lighton Synge, a mathematician from Dublin, had the monkeys sat again at a writing desk in 1957 – and to all of Shakespeare's theatre, tragedies and comedies, he added his poetry, the Bible, the Koran, along with any old poem written that morning by any human being found waiting for the bus.

In *The Case of the Midwife Toad*, published in 1972, Arthur Koestler mentioned a single *proverbial monkey*, the typewriter and a sonnet by Shakespeare: difficult to make it any simpler.

THE ANIMAL SCRATCHES HIS HEAD WITH HIS LEFT HAND

Those versions of the fable, it was inevitable, ended up reaching the ears of Samuel McIntosh, then mathematician or gardener, or both at the same time, as he was spending his time plucking the petals of daisies in order to solve the problems raised by Leonardo da Pisi (another mathematician). (His ears had always been large and developed, generous, greedy, in all the versions we collected: large enough to grapple with the latest music trend, large enough to hear how the algebraic science renewed its counting rhymes.)

He was a practical man, it was said: for him, abstractions were magnificent storm clouds – even more magnificent when they decide to descend once more on Earth and become incarnate, one way or another: as the cloud (this is an image) materialised sooner or later into rain, and the moment after into mud: a whole mess in which our boots get stuck. In the eyes of Samuel McIntosh, Albert Einstein's twins, of whom one had become older than the other, must well and truly be somewhere (in a farm in Ohio, for example: the oldest making the wood of an old rocking chair creak, the other out gallivanting). To have *The Divine Comedy* executed by a chimpanzee tied to a typewriter is for him an allegory, perhaps a gracious hypothesis, but above all else an experiment: something much more precious still. That's why, to all those purely hypothetical versions of the fable, Samuel McIntosh wanted to add his own, with the humility that is suitable for a gardener mathematician turned ethnologist: empirical versions, experienced versions, staged at the zoological gardens with the help of Percival (chimpanzee) and Remington (typewriter).

Chapter 6

THE ANIMAL HANGS FROM THE BRANCHES

How Percival the ape was captured: according to some versions, it was an epic capture, in Borneo: the dangers, the chase, the exploits of a great hunter coupled with a great zoologist, the white doctor lost in the primary forests, followed by a guide, preceded by a thousand mosquitoes, maintained by parasites, in daytime, in night time, straining his ears to the cries of the monkeys, howlers or not, while he kept waiting for the voice of *his* chimpanzee: the one which would be suitable. Or else (other versions), simple stories of trade: on the one hand the trader of chimpanzees (a dealer, a clandestine, at the border: he transports rare turtles and the last remaining lemurs); on the other, the buyer, the banknotes, the fixed price, no receipt — finally an ape trapped between those two human prattlers, an ape situated beyond, below, on top or underneath the hagglings.

To capture a chimpanzee, always 1.25 times smarter than his hunter: a whole trial — (if only it was a simple question of buying, on a Saturday morning, in the pet shop, amidst the cages for rabbits, guinea pigs, cats and dogs, all imploring, their eyes the mirrors of our own feelings of pity, looking sheepish, the muzzle so tempting, and let's not forget the goldfish, the parakeets, and that oh-so stretched ferret — if it was a question of that, only that, nothing would be simpler, it would have sufficed to rise at dawn to avoid the crowd, choose one's chimpanzee according to the sheen of its coat, consult its pedigree and medical certificate, look into the hollow of its ears to see the pearly aspect of healthy flesh, and go back home, a parcel under one's arm). To capture: not so simple, even, and above all, for a novice: first, get to know Borneo, differentiate between primary forest and secondary forest, read the signs, hear the cries, spot the habitats, move forward against the wind, display cunning stratagems, camouflage oneself, take on the most vegetal appearance possible, acquire by standing stock still, the discretion of a fern, progress with slowness and, above all, know one's prey: not be content with setting a trap between two trees, but get to know: when, where, how, why, according to which ceremonies and which paths, at what hour of dawn and in which circumstances. Know if the chimpanzee sleeps alone or in collective dormitories, if it ventures far from its relatives or remains hanging onto its mother's coat, if it sings, if it goes from branch to branch, if it walks on the ground, if it's shy, if it's pleasant, if it smiles and what it can possibly mean with that smile as exaggerated at first sight as the size of its arms.

By which miracle Borneo? — normally, no chimpanzee is spotted there, only orang-utans, legions of them (more and more sparse perhaps, but legions nevertheless): good-natured orang-utans leaning against branches, each its own, and giving, at the same time, an interpretation of the wild life, the after-meal nap and melancholy. For one third of the versions, examined closely through the eyes of the specialists, Percival is indeed an orang-utan, an adolescent, soon to be adult, suffering from an identity crisis like all of us suffer at that age: he dreams about beautiful destinies, the idea of belonging to an endangered species is unbearable to him; he prefers to think of himself as a chimpanzee, as he would see himself as a bonobo to diversify his pleasures for a change, or a porpoise so as to lark about in the sea. According to other versions, the capture happened in the Congo, logically, not far from the river — as for the remaining fables, they justify as best they can the presence of one single chimpanzee on an island in Indonesia: either exile, or signalling error, or the kidnapping of a new-born by a female of another species, or incredible chance, or chromosomal aberration like the black swan or the pink whale. McIntosh liked to see in that anomaly a kind of symbolism: the ultimate solitude, a chimpanzee in the land of orang-utans (he was spot on, that guy; for wasn't he living himself like an intruder amongst his peers).

According to rare and more dubious versions, the naturalist gardener avoids long journeys, and is quite happy to climb over the enclosure wall, to the zoological gardens, towards the pavilion of the great apes, to commit a bold burglary (lasso, capture, fox-trot, affray, kidnap), worthy of Munchausen and quite in his line, then to go back over the wall the other way. If he wants to show himself more Munchausen still, if he wishes a feat close to a miracle, instead of the lasso and the waltz he can undertake another form of rapture, through words: McIntosh comes across two ears attentive to his arguments in Percival the ape: he mentions career and heroic science and sings the praise of his Remington – Percival is undoubtedly seduced; you should see him nodding his head.

Chapter 7

THE ANIMAL REFUSES TO SET HIS MIND TO WORK [LAZING AROUND]

One would like to see him work with the same malleability – but of course, things don't always work as planned: in one of the very first versions of the fable arbitrarily numbered 1, Percival the chimpanzee, instead of tapping on the typewriter, accomplished a spin – a movement that conforms to the description given by the manuals of ethnology: *the subject moves the front part of his body, shifting around alternatively towards the left then the right, the back of his body always remaining fixed.*

Chapter 8

VARIOUS BEHAVIOURS, WHEEZE DANCE, SNIFF INSPECT, SHAKE, SWIPE, ETC.

In the second version of the fable, Percival the chimpanzee accomplishes a wheeze dance, defined as a to-and-fro motion without any direct relation to the sexual mount – itself generally accompanied by twitter, grunt and gargle.

In the third version of the fable, Percival the chimpanzee engages in an invitation to grooming, preceded by a sniff inspect, and followed by a tongue-out – the tip of the tongue eventually touching the chin.

In the fourth version of the fable, Percival the chimpanzee, perhaps feeling irritated (overwhelmed by the number of letters of the alphabet or the number of possible combinations or the extent of eternity), successively accomplishes a lolling of the head (headflag), a double threat (overlord), an open-mouthed/bared-teeth facial expression, a bounce and a shake – the fable specifies that after having accomplished the whole lot successively, Percival accomplishes it alternatively, then simultaneously, and finally, furiously.

(In the four (b) version, Percival the chimpanzee engages in three series of nine piloerections: obviously still frustrated.)

In the fifth version, Percival the chimpanzee, in association with another chimpanzee (Igrène), accomplishes a dance, classified in the category of Behaviours of Approach and Negotiation. The dance is composed of the following units: touch, spin, pacing, head tilt, duck face, wrinkly face, cheek-to-cheek threat, and, to finish it off, push, bounce, shake, swipe, wheeze, grunt, peep then gargle; it can be followed by a sexual mount.

In the sixth version, Percival the chimpanzee, still in the company of his partner Igrène, accomplishes one or several yawnings, from the category Other Behaviours and Activities.

According to the seventh version, Percival, facing his typewriter, maintains the stare attitude; the seven (b) version keeps the same system, rigorously the same, but replaces stare with sleeping in contact.

But according to the eighth version of the fable, it is now the laboratory assistant McIntosh's turn to perform a series of postures and actions all coming from the category Agonizing Behaviours: frown, swipe, hit, branch break, display posture and hammering. In the last paragraph of that version, Percival the chimpanzee associates the behaviour grin with looking backwards, twitter, and, never too late, typewriting.

Chapter 9

THE ANIMAL
JUMPS
OUT OF BED

In the ninth version of the fable, Percival the ape still has the freshness of a beautiful April dawn, optimistic first thing in the morning, ready to believe everything and pray to any divinity, including the divinity of guava, with a pure fervour. We can see him nicely combed, radiant, on his chair, in front of his typewriter; his coat is silky, it participates enthusiastically, no parasite would be found in it, flees or lice far removed from this story — it is dawn, everything shines, the typewriter at least as much as the chimpanzee, and between the two a basket of fruits. McIntosh, feeling younger too in that atmosphere of sprightly spring, is witness to that scene and enjoys with his eyes closed that art of being simple and direct. The arrangement is respected: an ape, a Remington, pure chance, pure luck and a master piece to compose; the still young Percival displays a tender docility, well and truly in the spirit of the fable, blindly optimistic, without obstacle: he is asked to apply chance, he applies it, he even incarnates it, he agrees to be a mechanism, to move his fingers at the service of large numbers. (But something is faulty, a small detail: from the very beginning, Percival presses with a single finger the same key, again and again, the *o*, out of desire for simplicity perhaps, a simplicity pushed to the very limit. Also hypnotised by that *o* which is forever repeating itself, McIntosh wonders if that juvenile mechanism of a chimpanzee is not corrupting chance, instead of serving it.)

Chapter 10

THE ANIMAL EXHAUSTS THE VARIOUS COMBINATIONS, AND VICE-VERSA

That's what the tenth version of the fable offers: at the beginning, the typist shows himself to be enthusiastic; the Remington is a toy, what it displays gleams, and then there is what it keeps secret, even more gleaming still; the keys glide, the oil is fresh, the hammers hit the page exactly at the right place, that's at least what appears to be – the Remington is a pleasure, it represents the mechanic when the mechanic functions like a dream, with no breakdown but with no excitement. Next to the table, the pyramids of blank paper are worth the mangroves, they are the beautiful promise and the carpet of white satin; and McIntosh, instead of being an algebraist embittered by his burden, is still a dashing young gardener in love with numbers, persuaded to castigate Fermat, one day, and to steal the glory of Linné on the same day. At the beginning, the eternity in front of him resembles the summer holidays and the law of large numbers flatters the typist: it promises the moon for one of these days – while he's waiting, thousands of combinations pass through thousands of reasons to live, thousands of possible existences, or scenarios of existences, as many objects of farce and meditation, to sum it up, he is spoiled for choice.

The good times, the golden age, the season of mirabelles – if only: the laws of probability which were so intoxicating at the very beginning, forecast upcoming, the exhaustion of opportunities, at the same time logical and cruel: after the hours of hope, a dreary eternity will follow, made of disenchantment, when the possibilities will become rare – the pile of white sheets will go down, every chance, good or bad, will dwindle; the typist ape, disillusioned by experience, will press down a key, then another, with less enthusiasm, with, on the contrary, the heaviness of a boxing match; the Remington will have the time to rust a few times and even go beyond rust, to catch up with the arthrosis of old mechanisms, that irony doesn't save. To know one has behind oneself most of the work accomplished, in the form of failed combinations, to know how chance or opportunity (delicious fairy dance) are reduced to very little, then nothing, is enough to make anyone taciturn, especially when the time comes to understand that the past, life itself, would only have been the exhaustion of all possibles, now classified according to an order of pertinence.

(It would have been the cramp, the breakdown, copper monoxide, a dead bulb above his head, the Remington's ribbon replaced by a flannel belt; Percival will no longer devote his hours to track down poetry at random, he will just calculate the probability for a young chimpanzee like himself to be chosen from among a hundred others: as soon captured, raised to the rank of a great writer: a stanza, a banana, a stanza.)

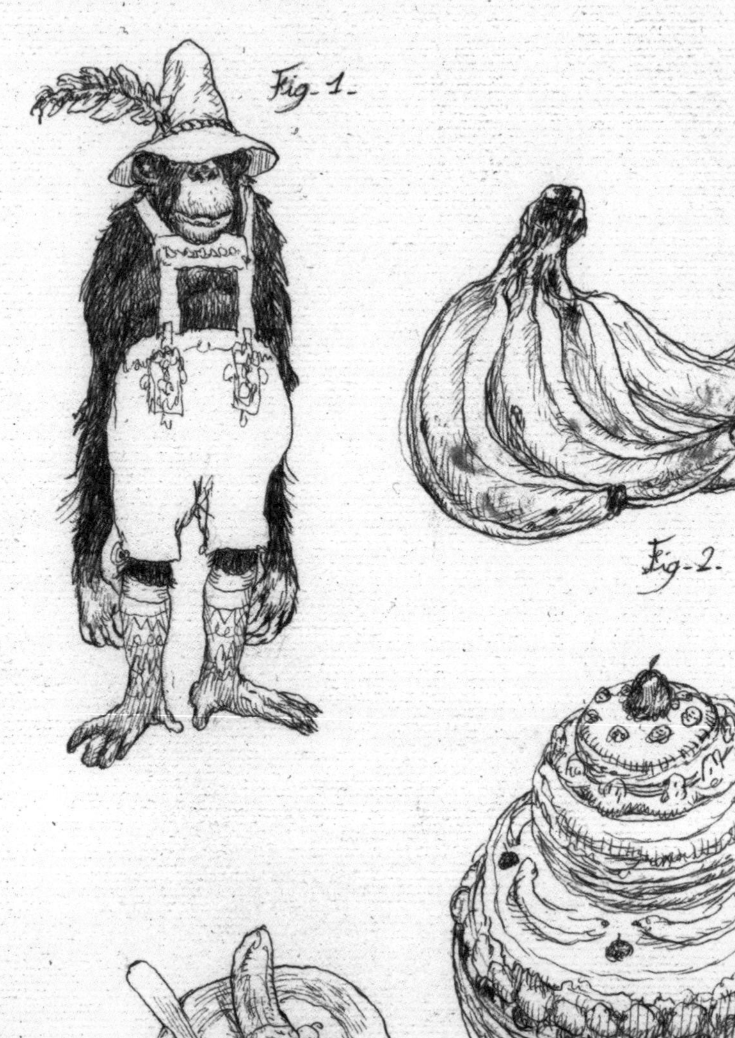

Fig. 1.
Fig. 2.
Fig. 3 bis.
Fig. 3.

Chapter 11

THE ANIMAL GROWS TIRED OF BANANAS; HE INVENTS GASTRONOMY

On an illustration of the tale torn from a book that's been lost, Percival, dressed up Tyrolean fashion, considers a peeled banana set on a plate looking, in a rustic way, like a tin dish (or a trough): it is probably an optical illusion, an effect of our own thought, but at that precise moment, Percival gives the impression of wanting to invent gastronomy: if only to have done with the banana, banana, banana, always the banana.

Chapter 12

THE ANIMAL
USES TOOLS

Way before lining up randomly three verses of a sonnet by Shakespeare, the Remington had the time to collapse a hundred times: it is a fragile mechanism, what one terms a delicate constitution. Inevitably, after the first twelve months of uninterrupted service, the keys of the first row work loose, the return bar oxidises, the base caves in, the *e* no longer leaves a mark, the *s* smudges and one learns to live without it, as one does with the commas and semi-colon; three times on five, from its hundredth hour or its hundredth day, the machine eats the paper: one can see there the metamorphosis of an office Remington into a meat mincer, screwed to the edge of the worktop.

The twelfth version of the fable offers a variation on the theme of craft: the chimpanzee, instead of writing, wonders how to improve that Remington decidedly too flimsy in spite of its impressive look as implacable grinder – nine times on ten unproductive.

Chapter 13

THE ANIMAL PULLS THE REMINGTON APART

The taste for the beautiful machine, especially when one pulls it apart (the passion for dismantling sometimes taking over the machine itself: one supposes that the enumeration of the parts is superior to an already sublime entirety). According to another version of the fable, the thirteenth, Percival the chimpanzee makes the most of an hour when he is not watched over (McIntosh paces up and down from courtyard to garden, singing softly, thinking of something else, as absent-minded as God in the Bible), to suspend his writing assignment: instead of typing, he pulls apart; he has brainwaves, which turn out to be destructive in the long run; he makes use of a twenty cents coin to unscrew the screws in the opposite direction to the hands of a watch; his intelligence in matters of craft has become sharp enough (sharper, it appears, as the Remington falls apart) to enable him to use now a piece of the machine, let's say the metal rod of the letter *z* as a particular tool, an extra one, useful either to unscrew the Remington a bit more (turn it on its back, invite it to reflect), or to clean his ears (mixing business with pleasure).

Chapter 14

THE ANIMAL MISLEADS THE REMINGTON

In some versions of the fable, the chimpanzee grows so attached to his machine that he covers it, curls up on it and suffocates it, as if he was sitting on an egg or a thimble – according to other versions Percival does it all except his duty: he is seen walking away, further away from the machine, performing around it a series of concentric circles that become increasingly wider, to the point of giving the Remington the part of a minute and negligible axis surrounded by a desert. According to the fourteenth version of the fable, the typist ape, under the gaze of his lab assistant, becomes interested in the machine again (the morning is drawing to an end, there have been difficult moments, instants of laziness, distraction, or boredom close to melancholy): he seems to make good use of it, McIntosh would admire that harmony between animal thought and mechanical efficiency – it all tallies, or almost: the Remington no longer seems to have as purpose the composition of Shakespeare's sonnets, but rather the cracking of an enemy's skull, for the moment invisible, indefinable too, a field mouse or a rat, or the last of the cockroaches: the Remington has become a simple bludgeon.

And when the machine is not used as some kind of weapon with a blade, according to the 14(b) version, it serves as a toaster: it's enough to bestow on Percival enough reasoning reason to convert in so few gestures a typewriter into a gracious toaster: almost the science of the anagram when it's all about combining the same elements following a different order (the good one, this time, this time it's certain). After what, according to that version of the fable, Percival forgets the work in progress, Shakespeare's sonnets, that depressing story of accomplishment through literature: no man ever made a living out of it, better to slice some bread and toast it (lunch time fast approaching, no more time to compose).

Chapter 15

THE ANIMAL EATS THE REMINGTON

The fifteenth version of the fable finds Percival in almost similar conditions: distraction of McIntosh, boredom combined with weariness, shortage of paper and perhaps of inspiration too, yearning for dismemberment in the foolish hope of understanding (as if *to understand* found its paradise in the space that separates the elements from one another), serene puerility and desire to bring to an end what has been started by chance (the dislocation). To which that fifteenth version adds: as he considers the totality of those spare parts on the carpet, some shiny, some matt, or round and square, or tubular and discoidal, Percival the chimpanzee sees them no longer as elements of a cold mechanism, but as an assortment of sweets, which gathers ecumenically crystallised fruits and hazelnut wafers – hunger counts for a lot in the process of analysis: tired of enumerating, Percival nibbles, how should we say?, admits the nibbles for nibbles, and while trying out various bits, ends up having his lunch.

Chapter 16

THE ANIMAL TEACHES LANGUAGE TO HIS TYPE–WRITER

According to the sixteenth version, Percival, leaning on his Remington, susceptible to its charm, its reflections, its oil and ribbon, a figure of eternity coiled on itself, Percival doesn't just press here or there with a cruelty which suits chance, but strokes the machine, pampers it, shows it an all too chimpanzean concern, a sensitivity only visible at the hour of delousing (imagine: seizing a louse between two boxing gloves). Leaning forward still, sticking out his lips, he even gives the impression of talking to it – a fraternal talk, made of twitters, moans, gargles, grunts, cries and sighs. To tell the truth, according to that version of the fable, Percival devotes his time to teaching the machine ape language: so that it expresses itself at least, for lack of truly speaking and for lack of writing the complete Shakespeare, starting with *As You Like It* – for it to express itself as a primate, one of the only languages Percival can understand and to which he would like to respond, just to feel in good company: it would be a mix of well-ordered clickings and symbols blackening the page. In a few hours, by sheer persistence, that damned Percival should reach his goal: but he needs to be given time, time for a pedagogue coming from his countryside to tame the machine – if one believes the fable in its sixteenth version (and the variants passed over in silence), night falls before he gets the slightest result (in a few other versions the chimpanzee triumphs, but his successes remain unpresuming, like his genius and his pride).

Chapter 17

THE ANIMAL
YAWNS

According to the seventeenth version, Percival the ape is bored — one has to admit it: to type for hours an incoherent series of letters is hypnotic (moreover, towards nine o'clock, the morning already appears to stretch endlessly). Writing is amusing sometimes, entertains or loosens the fingers, one could compare it to piano training — after *Hamlet*, the *Goldberg Variations* — and, every twenty seconds, a little bell announces the end of the line: it sounds like the chime of an old clock. But writing is not everything: as the sheets come out the carriage, one following the other, and unfold above the black and red ribbon, Percival has to act like a reader, after having acted like a typist: to read what comes out of his machine, without exception, judge, appreciate or not, get caught up in the suspense, if there is one, frown because he understands nothing, or yawn (he did yawn so many times), lose the thread, forget the name of the characters (are there really characters?), not give a monkey about their destiny, confuse the names and places, past and present. And as most of what comes out the carriage is a tireless series of 0 and 1, all his good will as a reader becomes exhausted, in a very short time — but the hope remains that the beginning of a story will come to replace boredom with the pleasure of the tale: it wouldn't be the first time that a story delivers the reader not only of his or her weariness, but of all pointless discourses.

Chapter 18

THE ANIMAL EXPERIENCES BOREDOM

Percival, an apprentice in boredom, one among all human feelings, sometimes has the impression of knocking himself out on a monotonous piano: if the 84 black and white keys of his keyboard only made a C sharp, then the music would be even less entertaining than the front door bell. If at least the fable in its eighteenth version allowed him to write, while anticipating Shakespeare's sonnets, one or two detective novels, with the twists and turns of a good plot, just to take his mind off things — he would have the strength to wait until the advent of his Great Work, with, under his eyes, as he plans them, the adventures of a detective confronted with stories of locked rooms (and the glass of poisoned wine, and the mysterious window, and the howl of the dog at five to midnight, and the falsified will, and the culprit found dead, and the left shoe without the right, the complicated timetables, the alibis much too ingenious, and in the middle of all those calculations, the blade of a knife, a particularly nasty open wound, the blue clashing with the red).

Chapter 19

THE ANIMAL
WAITS FOR
HIS FELLOW APES

In the nineteenth version, McIntosh curses his fate, neglects his duty, regrets not to be, for example, one of Arthur's knights on one of the pages of Chrétien de Troyes: simple figurehead perhaps, not much, but the chance to go into the woods, eat wild strawberries, follow in its coil the sound of a crumhorn and finally visit the charming ladies from a bygone age, with their transparent veils and unlaced virtue, if necessary. (If not one of Arthur's knights, then a chimpanzee from the bonobo family, famous libertines, and refined though rustic: so that at least he would feel all perked up instead of wasting his energy sorting out the consonants, so that at least his performances in bed would be studied, instead of his mediocre intelligence: as combination, he would happily forget the 26 letters of the alphabet in order to exhaust the 16 postures of Aretino, followed by the 8 bites from the *Sutra* of Vatsyayana.)

Of course the original device was elegant – a single machine, a single ape, a monument dedicated to literature –, but elegance doesn't take into account boredom, no more than solitude (and those idle times, the sadness associated with solitude, shared half and half between human brothers and primate cousins): mathematics don't give a toss about that solitude, as they don't give a toss about the rings around Uranus, full of titanium dust. To attract fellow creatures, Percival did his utmost, he proved to have much imagination by waving his arms about, shaking off his sweat, using a vocabulary one didn't suspect he had: he evoked the joys of company, he wished to convey the idea that a disciplined troupe of six or seven chimpanzees, up for a chat, just the necessary amount, could save him from suffering from isolation: like colleagues, they would from time to time look up from their keyboards, they would rest their typists' old bones with the faint laughter that follows stupid jokes; they would sometimes launch into songs of galley slaves, canon and fugue, as far as the coda, before falling silent by mutual agreement — and from that silence, they would fully benefit. McIntosh himself, the eighth of a group of seven, would appreciate the company of the primates; he would encourage them by turning the small handle of a music box, adding his voice to their voices, discordant but full, watching over the apes as over an office full of unruly university graduates. Each evening, after the writing session, he would invite them for a drink at the zoo's cafeteria, where some colleagues meet up, naturalists, ethologists, wearing white blouses, or grey, and glaring at the apes.

Chapter 20

THE ANIMAL
CHOOSES
HIS COMPANY

The twentieth version of the fable sees Percival walking in the zoological gardens, moving towards the pavilion of the great apes: he neglects the proboscis monkey with its preacher's face, the academy of orang-utans, the gorillas with their black leather, comes close to the chimpanzees, and there undertakes an extensive game of seduction until five, then six of them, so the fable recounts, jumps over the barriers, joining Percival and his typewriter, and his promise of a Great Work. (Some versions are more flattering than others: especially this one, number 20(b), in which Percival stands out like no one, makes his coat shiny, shows himself handsome both full-on and in profile. His coat of chimpanzee troglodyte, instead of being a proof of negligence, is a discreet fantasy, downy, linear like Clark Gable's moustache; one could think him naked, such is his refusal to give way to hirsutism, through elegance – he already subjugates, it's true, three of four females, puts them in his pocket so to speak, between them he could choose [but he doesn't choose, through, as always, his concern for elegance – that was supposed to make him attractive]. Returning to the laboratory, to the typewriters, accompanied by six others, in his image, he is tactful enough not to proclaim himself master of the little troupe: he proves to be discreet, on the contrary, lets things follow their course, since chance demands it, chance and a certain detachment.)

Chapter 21

THE ANIMAL
CONVERSES

All gathered in one single room, according to the twenty-first, twenty-second and twenty-third versions of the fable: which implies memorable bouquets, if only one could smell them: heady, musky, odours from Borneo added to those of Tanzania and the zoos of Western Europe – which also implies a sane competitiveness between fellow creatures, all scribes, all provided with a keyboard: if one of them started to play the harmonica, the company would begin to dance, and vice versa. Percival is no longer alone, he experiences the team spirit, as in the historical versions of the fable composed by Raymond Lulle (three macaques), or Emile Borel (a million chimpanzees: it would be a miracle to contain them all in one single room, it would be another miracle to feed them without provoking jealousy); he appreciates the company, he makes the most of it, as if he knew how other more austere versions chose to leave him alone, with, for sole partner, that lab assistant who falls asleep and forgets to play the ham opposite. According to 23(b), coming directly out of the twenty-third, Percival typewrites, each time more precise in the choice of his keys and the strength of his tapping, in order to start with his fellows a conversation, in a percussive mode, in a language that should resemble Morse code – or let's say ragtime. According to the 23(c) version, coming from the 23(b), Percival abandons the Morse code, too rudimentary at that moment in his story (how to say?, beneath the capacities of an ape now taking on Shakespeare, familiar with his writing and rhetoric): he prefers to devote himself to the pleasure of correspondence: one should picture here the sweet nothings made of fifty or so signs, each note passing from one table to the next; it keeps friendship alive, and sometimes spreads, in the shape of a written joke, a kind of primate humour, pan-troglodyte, close to our humour — (we would laugh about the same absurdities, the same ridiculous things and the same shortcuts [Samuel McIntosh believes], if only we could laugh at the same time, by respecting the same grammar of laughter).

Chapter 22

THE ANIMAL
MOURNS

Those fellows, the twenty-fourth version of the fable gives them a name: Manfred, Conrad, Orson, Diane, Ophelia, Zoe – in that exact order, or inexact, depending on Percival's memories: by seeing those letters dance in front of his eyes and hypnotise him, his ape's brain does not always let him remember who he is. How then to sort truth from falsehood: is it really Manfred who succumbed to tuberculosis after six weeks of an incredible racket (a cough) over his carriage? Or was it Conrad? But wasn't Conrad that chimpanzee from Sumatra, too young to overcome the ordeal, too nervous, shaken by mystical impulses, his eyes two slices of mango, always praying to his great primate gods, loudly, no laughing matter, which used to put Ophelia, who was sitting next to him, in a complete state (until he finally croaked and shut up for the first time in his life). And wasn't Orson that lanky ape who had shot up in Holland, in the hot houses of a zoo, so lean he looked like a marmoset, still thinner in the corpse state, folded in eight behind the toilet door in the posture of a carpenter's folding ruler? As for Zoe, she was perhaps that female ape with hazelnut eyes and a sad face who managed to put aside for three months enough bitter almonds to successfully attempt a suicide with Prussic acid one evening in June – and Diane, wasn't she that girl who lost all appetite: first her appetite for bananas and then her appetite for life? God knows… (Whoever she was, Diane or Zoe, Ophelia didn't survive her for long, she who used to sing even Duke Ellington's airs and Fred Astaire's songs: nothing more jolly than that.) (According to that version of the fable, collective writing didn't last long: six months later at most, there was nobody left, the subtraction is an elementary operation devoid of pity – nobody left apart from Percival, at least him, the last among them, and the irremovable McIntosh [much grief, but enough composure to go and sell to the bric-a-brac traders six Remingtons in good nick and six real pelts – to feed seven chimpanzees had cost him quite a bit].)

Chapter 23

THE ANIMAL GOES FROM TEARS TO LAUGHTER

The twenty-fifth version is a story of mourning and burials: one lost count of the number of vets coming to verify that the sack of fur crowned by a heavy head is no longer anything more than a sack of fur. All those dead bodies in so little time make Percival melancholic, his prose suffers from it, even though it is due only to chance: one shall eventually succeed one day in making connections between painful mourning and random combinations. He is only left with burying the dead, forgetting them, regaining his joy for living, and if he doesn't manage that, rebuilding it from scratch: by playing with words, or with knucklebones, for example: looking for distraction after the mourning.

The fable in its twenty-sixth version had done with requiems: the mourning is far away, the earth settles down on top of Diane and Zoe, the chimpanzee's grief gradually transforms into a general melancholy, with no cause, with no precise term, more and more diluted, until disappearing – then the noise of the typewriter is reminiscent of a calypso for a seafront ball, a calypso devoid of the smallest feeling of culpability.

Chapter 24

THE ANIMAL
SLEEPS, SNORES, STRETCHES, SHRIVELS

In the twenty-seventh version, the time has come for naps: that of Percival (bushy, it is gathered on itself), that of Samuel McIntosh (stiffened, uncomfortable on a stool), that of the Remington (one would like to see it puffing and panting like a 1930 Ford after a steep climb and descent in the Rocky Mountains). If Samuel McIntosh is the first to wake up, he finds in the middle of the room the pile of sleepy fur of his ape: looking at it from afar, he can only guess a pile, indeed, devoid of any meaning as of any direction, bum and head here or there, wherever — by looking closer, McIntosh cannot stop himself from thinking that there is here, in that distinct indecision, that of a cushion, an eiderdown, or a tuft, a certain pertinent something, perhaps the sign or the outline of a sign — closer still and McIntosh would understand that his chimpanzee Percival doesn't content himself with sleeping, but interprets the sleeper, suggests the sleepiness, signifies the sleep and doesn't stop wanting to sleep by saying *I sleep* in each snoring noise coming from his nostrils — closer still and this time McIntosh could get an interest in the language of fleas. (On the day when, unfortunately Percival the chimpanzee will die, having used all his energy, exhausted by the sheer fact of undertaking a Great Work which never ever would have seen the light of day, he will perhaps have become clever enough, clever in the human sense of the term, to not be content with just being dead, but miming the

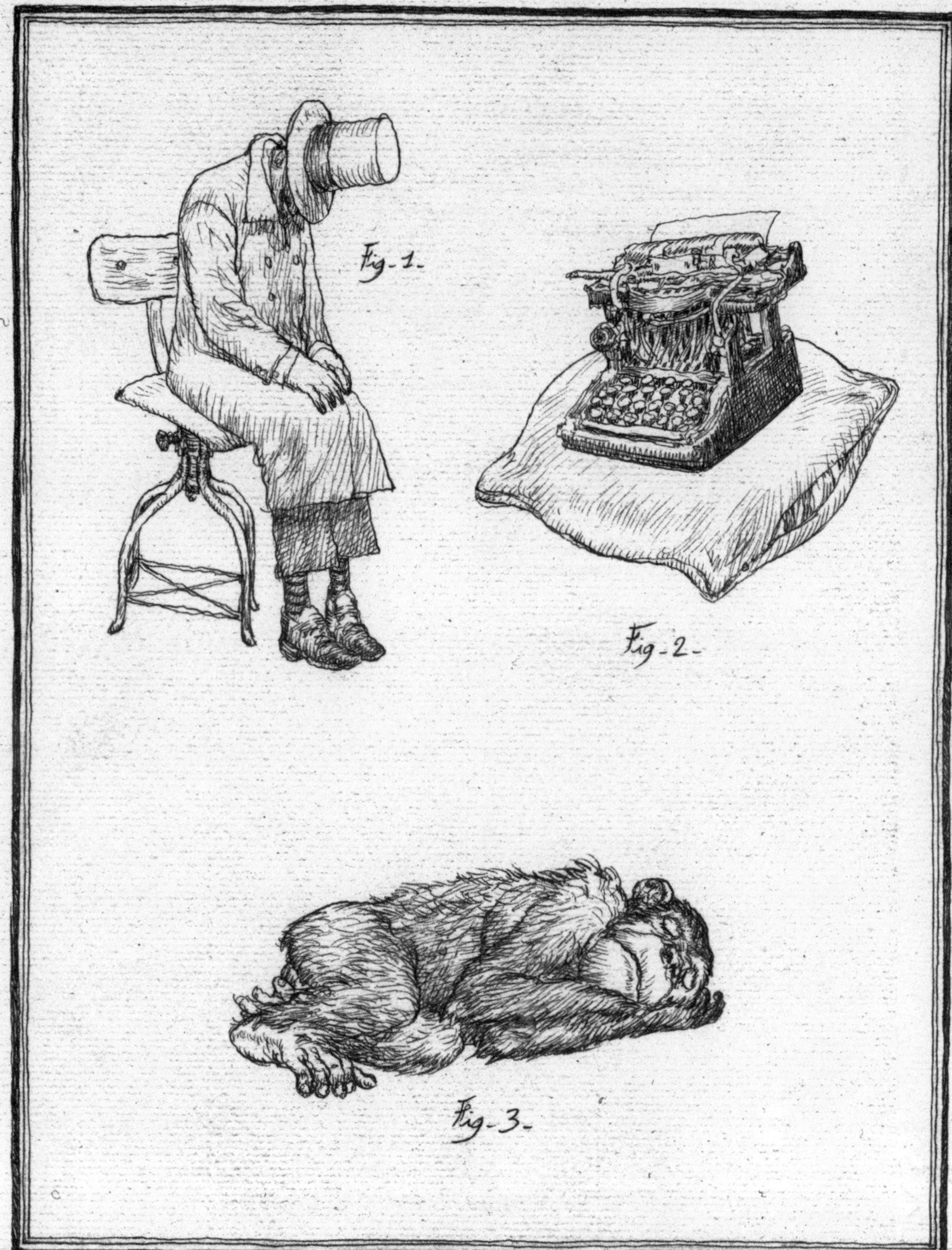

Fig. 1.
Fig. 2.
Fig. 3.

corpse, and interpreting the dead with all the *savoir faire*, all the culture acquired during those long months of writing – and by rubbing shoulders with (and imitating) McIntosh, he would have, now, the sense of the funeral, as one learns the art of partying and a sense of humour.)

Chapter 25

THE ANIMAL MULTIPLIES THE VERSIONS

We can't go through a list of all the variations of the fable: many are needless repetitions, many ring hollow, and we have read false ones too, ridiculously false ones, we also know some that lose their way with a misleading determination, but without ever taking the reader with them, fortunately – the cautious reader anyway. The versions are not infinite, that would take one's fantasies for a mathematical reality – but a certain number of clues lead us to believe that they still proliferate today, at the time those lines are written, and won't stop before all other forms of narration have been silenced. They use the words chimpanzee, baboon, orang-utan, Olivetti and Underwood; they evoke Shakespeare's sonnets or his complete works (comedies, tragedies, historical dramas) or the British Museum, sometimes the Warburg library, while waiting for vaster Ali Baba caves classified in alphabetical order; they are transmitted orally, that's why they are so easily lost on the way. Some have the jovial tone of Goldoni, some are dreadful in the ill-fitting settings of Kafka, where all the squares are in reality trapeziums, some are caustic like satires that would single out the species of journalists, others are sensitive, almost grief-stricken, others laconic, funny but disparaging, several succeed in handling Carroll's algebraic invention without sacrificing their characters made roaming like a whole flora and fauna of jumping-jacks and puppets, some unfinished, some definitive, and others precious as if they had been sketched, just sketched, way before the invention of the Remington, at the time of quilts and inkwells, when libertines were still pondering about the structure of the sofa and the physiognomy of the orgasm compared to the sofa.

In the boxes of rejected fables (useless versions: either paraphrases, or betrayals), one can find a few Grand Guignol narratives: one discovers Percival the ape battering, allegorically, but also in reality, his master McIntosh with the typewriter, until each of the letters of his keyboard prints (one is quoting from memory here) a particular form of death on his medical student's skull. Another makes of Percival an old chimp dragged too late in front of his Remington, as if he was asked to write his memoirs urgently: an old ape pursued by amnesia, apathetic, worn out (a touch of alopecia, a touch of what's the use), his final strength gathered in order to manage his final naps.

Chapter 26

THE ANIMAL SPELLS THE LETTERS OF HIS NAME

The twenty-eighth version of the fable: McIntosh waits for the moment he will witness a spectral *Hamlet* appear after a series of *frhtgfru* repeated since the day before, the day before the day before, the days before too: *Hamlet* as a narrative will end up summoning itself with the discretion of a discoloured ghost, silent, wearing slippers; it will appear in the form of a name, perhaps the name of Hamlet himself, or in the form of a reply, *words, words,* or a syllable, one of the sonorous syllables of Rosencranz, for example – at that moment, the chimpanzee, relieved, happy, as if he was seeing a friend coming along, will consider himself a freed creature: instead of dying of boredom in that enclosed room, he will at least be able to read the adventures of the King's son being murdered, the ones he is at present improvising on his typewriter. If the name of Hamlet doesn't appear, refuses to appear, because it is a timid ectoplasm, it will be the name of Beatrice, and *The Divine Comedy*, and if it's not Beatrice, then it will be Gulliver or *Wonderland*. And if it's neither Hamlet, nor Beatrice, nor Alice, if it's not the capture of Lilliput, then it will be the story of a chimpanzee sitting in front of his typewriter, or a portrait of that chimpanzee, the spiritual and physical portrait of a nice boy with soft brown hair, bright eyes and tough skin: the spitting image of Percival – and if it's not his portrait, nor his misadventures, then it will be thousands of signs on one single page to practise spelling the letters of one's name.

Chapter 27

THE ANIMAL TYPES THE LETTERS OF HIS NAME COMPOSES HIS SELF–PORTRAIT THEN HIS AUTOBIOGRAPHY

During the twenty-ninth version of the fable, slightly shorter than the others, Percival masters the keyboard of his Remington enough (let's be clear: he doesn't master chance, not even a primitive model of chance, but the machine) to write his name, in the middle of a page, starting with a capital P.

In the course of the thirtieth version, Percival no longer types his name (for he is called Manfred and has a red coat), but his self-portrait, skilfully polished off in sixteen lines, roundly and soundly done, in which one can guess an irony owing entirely to his intelligence, nothing left to the random combination of letters.

In the course of the thirty-first version, the chimpanzee typist is called neither Percival nor Manfred but Murphy; his coat is light brown, he has a scar shaped like an S on his forearm: he doesn't type his name in a line, nor his self-portrait in sixteen, but an autobiography, a whole autobiography in thirty-seven: it begins in Borneo, among the ferns, and ends, provisionally, in a white room, facing a typewriter, its fifth wall — it explains in the meantime the scar in an S shape: a story of love, drunken excess, unfaithfulness, jealousy and bad luck.

Chapter 28

THE ANIMAL PROVES TO BE MISCHIEVOUS

Percival will overcome *The Divine Comedy*, if it means to write *The Three Musketeers* instead: he will just have to brilliantly prove after that (if he can do a mid-air somersault, he can be brilliant) that *The Three Musketeers* is a preferable form of *Divine Comedy*: the more difficult the proof, the more flamboyant his triumph, like the holy chastity of Saint Augustine after years of free love and dirty beard. That will be, after a final full stop, the precise hour of his victory: he will remove the sheet from the typewriter, surprised not to see it flapping its wings and take off, before landing on a shoulder. [*A paragraph traditionally attached to the thirty-first version.*]

Chapter 29

THE ANIMAL
INTERPRETS

The thirty-second version of the fable shows Percival the chimpanzee busy reading his drafts: what does it matter if those drafts are a succession of x or y, or dots like lines of chick peas, he re-reads them, he devotes his time, showing concentration (seriousness, know how, etc), and swinging as only monkeys can do between indulgence and severity. The setting is the same, perhaps one can add an indoor plant to make things more comfortable – Percival seems to clear himself a path between those rows of x, y and chick peas. Fruitless hours, one would swear to it, hours spent for nothing – only the thirty-second version reassures us of the opposite: leaning this way, Percival discovers another pleasure, that of interpreting his own signs: and he succeeds, he derives from it a certain satisfaction, diffuse, still difficult to recognise, but soon also given to interpretation. After what, to come full circle regarding his reasoning, or to make the fun last, he enters episodes of introspection, like the reading of the lines on his hands (a little while later, he will be able to sneeze and find a meaning to his sneezing, and later still, yawn, "the most naturally in the world", but understand that those jaws, distant from one another, and the tongue lost somewhere between the two are a reproach addressed to his master McIntosh: the expression of boredom and the beginning of rebellion).

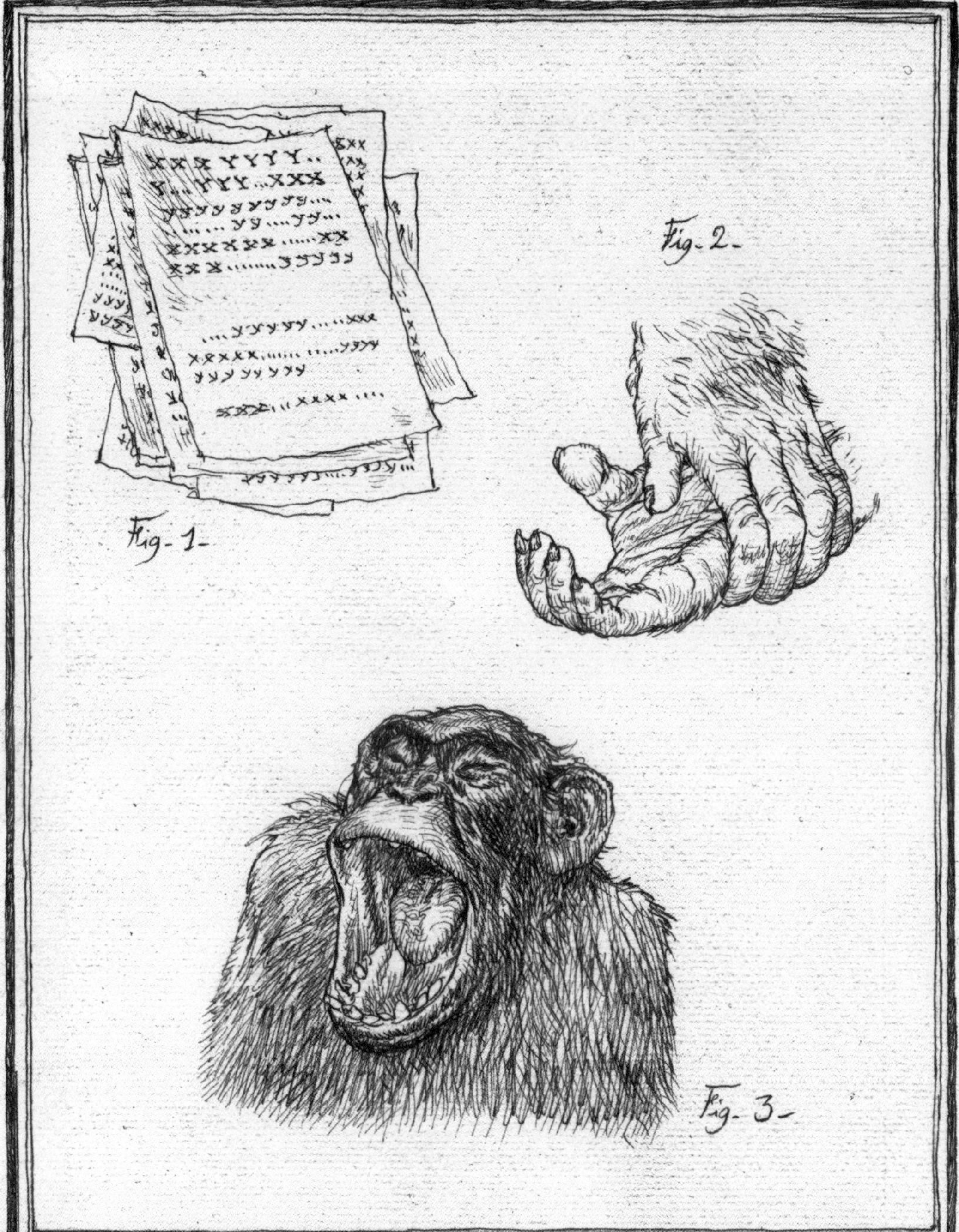

Fig. 1.
Fig. 2.
Fig. 3.

Chapter 30

THE ANIMAL
MIMICS

Imitation as second nature – (according to the 32(b) to 32(e) versions, not retained for lack of space, McIntosh spends a few hours wondering if it's enough to mimic the chimpanzee to become one, and if imitation is necessary, including when one was born under a tropical foliage as is a true chimpanzee, in a family of real primates). According to the thirty-third version, Percival, still scrupulously ape-like (one could have written *spectacularly*) leans over his Remington; he devotes to it the energy of a young ape, all the strength available since he no longer has to break nuts in two nor climb to the top of trees: he could have seen in the neighbourhood young typists, themselves focused on their pages: he types, he makes the typewriter shake, the result is no longer important, the essence being to play his part, which is to accomplish the gestures while putting the least irony into the act – the art of exact copy presupposes the greatest seriousness.

According to the thirty-fourth version, Percival the ape mimics a secretary in the era of the mechanical keyboard – according to the thirty-fifth version, Percival mimics McIntosh who himself mimics the PhD student, absorbed by his figures, his gravity, his protocol, his articles and reputation – according to the thirty-sixth version, Percival mimics the Remington with more talent still, more accuracy: its mechanisms, its articulation, plasticity, resistance, its faculty for obedience and for proving to be reticent, its reflections and parts, its pre-war elegance and humility as a tool – according to the thirty-seventh version, Percival, tired of imitating what surrounds him, would like to go over the wall to find again, behind, a whole world to freely ape: to ape as one recognises, and embraces.

Chapter 31

THE ANIMAL'S REFUSAL

Refusal (the art of refusing) is not unknown to animals: one remembers historical refusals that have become famous in our repertoire and made popular by proverbs: the stubbornness of the ass for example, *heehaw* meaning *never ever*, at the foot of a steep slope. Some refusals are particular to men, perhaps: like, let's say, the refusal of honours by a vain person – in this case a complex refusal, a refusal denying itself, decorated with a whole garland of lies. Sophisticated forms of refusal would permit the creature to encounter the object with a different alternative than rubbing against it (sniffing it, touching it with the tip of his tongue, or biting it as one does with a nickel dime [91.67% copper – 8.33% nickel]): pronouncing clearly *no*, for example, would be sufficient, or turning one's back on the thing, which prompts him to make an abstract idea out of it, circling it like a predator. The thirty-eighth version of the fable represents him (Percival) like that, on his two bum cheeks, trusting them with all his weight, his balance and determination facing his Remington: arms folded, sulking, stubborn like the ass earlier, inflexible judging by his frown: the experience can wait, chance will do without him, the ape refuses, simply, to hell with the banana – if he had to spell a single word, it would be n - o (why make it complicated?).

In the thirty-eighth version, a pyrographic illustration shows a McIntosh aged by exhaustion, despair and exasperation: a kind of Gepetto pulling out his last hair – one can see him rummaging through his library (*Animal Play Behaviour*, Oxford University Press, 1981, *Reading into Thought: The Minds of the Great Apes*, Cambridge

University Press, to maintain a sense of balance, 1996), making theses and bags of peanuts fall from them in the hope (one supposes) of understanding why that devil of a monkey of an ape is starting to play up – (McIntosh should have read instead: *The opposition phase in the 2 year-old child*, Psychiatry Now, vol XXII, 1974).

(According to the 38(b) version, the refusal is shared equitably, fifty-fifty, between Percival the subject and McIntosh his lab assistant: only the Remington seems to incarnate the whole positivity of acceptance, as if the *yes* shone in its parts: it remains there, inert but incorruptible, purely positive, fully aware of all the possibilities it contains – while it rejoices, and reflects the room's neon lights, Percival and McIntosh have already left: having run away from their work, they went in search of a pineapple (the fruit, not the incendiary).

Chapter 32

THE ANIMAL POSES

In the thirty-ninth version of the fable, Percival is standing, once again, next to the Remington, without even leaning against it, as a gentleman would on the taxidermy of a leopard, to pretend he killed it: he doesn't express his refusal, nor his weariness, he is not sulking, doesn't show any sign of exhaustion, there isn't in him, so it seems, an ounce of aversion – the aversion of the primate coming from his wild forest regarding intellectual things and that curio of a machine for novelists. No: out of reach of his typewriter, Percival becomes finally aware of his writer's destiny (speaking of destiny, let's add: *writer's vocation* to writer's nature and *author's rights*): he is standing up, he is right to do so (there is something of the artist already in the biped), he admires at the same time the keyboard, its reflections, and himself in the reflections, as well as his drafts in a pile next to the banana skins, tone on tone. He has become clever enough, sharp enough and advanced in his knowledge of the trade of novelist to know that the writer-being is not limited to the act of writing (for example the composition of the *Wives of Windsor*...), but presupposes a vast repertoire of gestures and mimicries accomplished far from the work table. The last chapters of the fable, without its thirty-ninth version, show how Percival, aware of what it means to have become a novelist (poet) adopts a brooding and elegant look; appears sagacious, puffs out his breast, combs his hair, takes care of his nails and seduces young girls, using his inspiration as the attribute of great breeding animals.

Chapter 33

THE ANIMAL
AWAITS INSPIRATION

One can't hear any clicking in the fortieth version: the machine doesn't ring, besides, the pages don't fill up, and the lab assistant doesn't spend his evenings filing in folders the drafts of the day, of various thicknesses depending on the weather (there is no rough draft). Instead of observing his chimpanzee in the posture of the typist, numb to the point of stretching his hand towards the chariot's handle each time the bell rings, McIntosh observes him the whole day, the entire day, motionless on his chair in the so stupefying attitude of the inspired poet. The Remington could rust in front of him, he would not even glance at it, he will persist in lying in wait for nothing, his nose in the air, but his forehead heavy. Such is the posture of the inspired poet: listening to the world's sadness, but keeping his mouth shut, a mark of scepticism, as if any sadness was not worth taking into account.

McIntosh doesn't say a word, he continues to have, at a fixed time, his three sandwich meals a day (letting the gherkins drop on his shoes is his way to contribute to the confusion); but nothing annoys him more violently than those fads of the young dude of an ape who labels himself poet. It exasperates him: to see those precious minutes fly by (the time t) and the days, while Percival doesn't move a single hair, thinking himself, in turn, Verlaine (on Monday), Mallarmé (on Tuesday), James Joyce (on Wednesday), T.S. Eliot (on Thursday), then, higgledy-piggledy Cummings, Hölderlin, Nerval and, we start all over again with Verlaine, still with his nose in the air, his chin between thumb and index, the stillness of the keeper of empty things punctuated with long sighs, which should say enough but doesn't mean much (McIntosh almost believed, during this fortieth version of the fable, that all poetry was nothing but the inspired translation, brilliant in the psychiatric sense, of boredom in versification).

Chapter 34

THE ANIMAL HAS INTENTIONS

Idleness knows of a thousand avatars, places, decors and postures – in other words, there is a thousand ways to laze around depending on motivations, reasonings, meanings and cultures (perhaps some remains of social utopias, or makeshift faith screwed to fear, or logic nailed to ancient, floating mysticisms). During the many versions of the fable (forty-one to forty-seven), Percival, unfaithful to his vocation as secretary mechanic, almost running away from his Remington, comes closer to the couch, settles there, we see his hominid's talent for lazing about blossoming – he doesn't accomplish anything precise, let's say anything humanly determinable (neither entirely *this*, nor entirely *that*), but if one looks closer, appears really and truly *to have intentions*: that gives him the look of a cat on the verge of pouncing on a field mouse seen by nobody except himself, a field mouse which didn't exist a minute earlier, and to which capture and death will give in an instant total credit. (It must be a form of intelligence, that idleness of monkeys always on the brink of going into action, containing his energy, totally engrossed in the effort of choosing how and in what direction to act, or towards which bunch of bananas – as if the intention was a supreme form of mischief, mischief when it becomes meditative, and aspires to more precious aims beyond bunches, beyond sweets: the fulfilment of a life or, to say it with emphasis, the unfolding of a being in space and time.

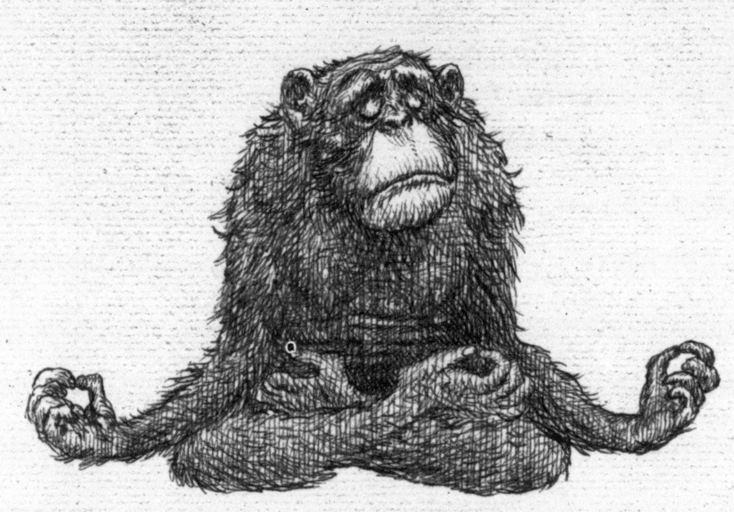

Fig. 1.

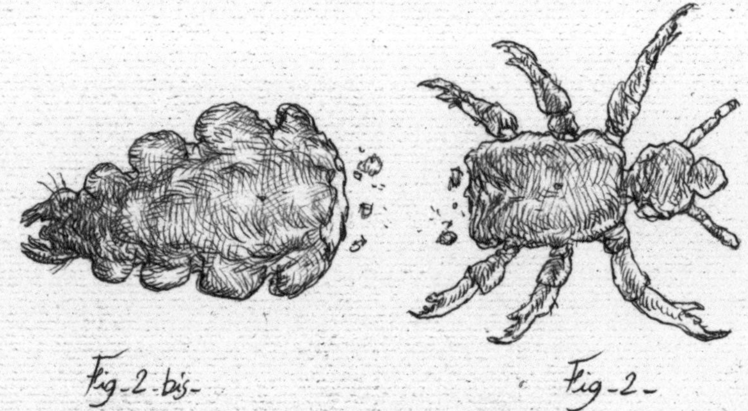

Fig. 2. bis.   Fig. 2.

Chapter 35

THE ANIMAL
ENGAGES
IN GROOMING

Banana as fruit and as meaning: fable forty-eight demonstrates how McIntosh acquires a taste for bananas: borrows them from his colleague, peels them, digests them, estimates with a single glance their maturity, evokes the pelts of big cats, immerses himself in their ever so peculiar flesh – so perfect a flesh that it must be restorative and constitute a part of ourselves. Fable forty-nine is crepuscular, softly crepuscular: Percival the typist shows himself to be courageous still in spite of the late hour (he would have munched on coffee grains, taking them for a variety of beetle); as for McIntosh, he has surrendered for a few minutes already to the lethargy of intellectuals seduced, then charmed, finally hypnotised by the pages of their book, the material pages: the pages turned one after another, like the slowest of fans. A man (*sapiens sapiens*) asleep, if he is sitting, obeys the same laws as some trees once cut down, there is no reason why it shouldn't be so: submitting to gravity, he leans, then falls: that's what McIntosh is doing, on his right side: and that's why fable forty-nine has him resting on his chimpanzee's knees, an abandon of grandson to his grand-dad: one of them snores, I mean gives himself with parsimony to snoring and deep sleep; the other stays awake, rolls eyes at the same time aperitif and compassionate, as if it was possible to mix fondness for sweet things with sympathy: one then sees him dropping the keyboard and undertaking within McIntosh's scholarly mop of hair, a session of grooming all the more intense for there isn't any louse to be found at the place one looks for them.

Chapter 36

THE ANIMAL DESCRIBES THE VIRTUES OF DELOUSING

Meditating is good, it's undoubtedly prophylactic, good for the whole organism, more or less the equivalent of a purgative with wild herbs, and it thins the blood, especially that which flows through the thin blood vessels between the cranium and the grey matter – meditating Cartesian-like is even better (or it should be): also purgative, emetic, anthelmintic, enough to unfold a bit more the alveoli of the lungs and have the lymph circulate there where it should. And then Cartesian meditation puts certain ideas back in place, it is as salutary as to relocate a vertebrae (barely painful – afterwards, a kind of voluptuousness, comparable to a couch): it firms up, it sows doubts, temporarily, makes one frown slightly, embarks the meditative in the dark corridors of reasoning where me, myself and I, intelligence, God and modelling clay are what matters. For the human, *sapiens sapiens sapiens*, and I'm leaving some out, Cartesian meditation can be a good thing, undoubtedly – I barely dare to pronounce on the matter, nor to meddle in something that's got nothing to do with me, or perhaps obliquely: there are so many dark thoughts, obscure feelings and even more obscure intentions in the short hair men that I give up looking for the birth of coherence (coherence in the ape-like meaning of the term), choosing to keep to simple schemes (they explain it all, or almost): hunger, thirst, love, hate, desire for glory and what's-the-point-ness. For the chimpanzees of my species (my kind, my family), Cartesian meditation can quite agreeably accompany naps, or begin, prolong or interrupt them – but it is not always enough: in a way it's much better to engage in delousing, it is in the Cartesian continuity a form of supreme meditation: parsimony is found there, as is the concern for distinguishing (distinguishing for example what is from what is not, and amongst what is, what is a louse from what is not a louse – it is the whole rigour of Parmenides resumed in a single gesture); there can be found doubts, sublimated, transcended through faith (in the efficiency of our gestures), a way to resolve immemorial enigmas about the being, the self, the self being and the knowing being. Delousing, to sum it up, if it's really a question of squeezing a minuscule dot between thumb and forefinger, then deciding, in spite of its fondness for our skin and its blood saturated with ours, deciding it is not part of ourselves, not even a tubercular or pustular part, as would be a cold sore, but entirely different, something else or better, someone else, to whom one must be able to give a name, show some respect and whom we assume has a deliberate conscience – if delousing is that hygienic and sometimes nourishing distinction between the *self* and the *non-self*, it is a part of philosophy: besides, nothing stops us thinking that at the time of being submitted to delousing, the louse itself does not meditate, articulating in its very own way its *therefore I am*, before disappearing, cut into two equal sections.

Chapter 37

THE ANIMAL DESCRIBES THE VIRTUES OF DELOUSING [2]

Delousing is a light meal, a polite phrase, an introspection through another being, a sincere desire to get to know, a psychoanalysis, simple compassion devoid of all sermon and all transcendence, an exercise in mental arithmetic, and the application on an object at arm's reach (in other words, *corpus*) of the desire for searching.

Delousing is a light meal: that's no mystery, it's the type of revelation so obvious that it necessarily hides others, a whole catalogue in fact: for the moment we are happy with comparing delousing to the aperitif hour, and the louse to a peanut: one finds there the same desire for passing one's time, staving off one's hunger and boredom, keeping one's fingers busy, in other words giving oneself a composure, and initiating through nibbling a beginning of... how do you say it?... socialising.

Delousing is a polite phrase: to not delouse one's fellow would amount to not greeting one another in the corridors of the department for Probabilities and Animal Behaviour; and I know of refined gorillas, slightly aloof, almost snobbish, who have chosen to remain full of lice so as to not have to submit to a grooming by their peers: to remain louse-ridden was a form of keeping-to-oneself.

Delousing is an introspection: because the top of my head and a great part of my back are the most difficult body parts to discover (with my soul, my deep self and the true worth of my sex appeal), if I don't manage to know myself, remains the illusion of going to meet my fellow creature, to embrace him like a brother, like a copy of myself, and to discover him in the same way, as a mirror: then, to untangle the hairs by tufts, then by lines, and hunt for the louse is not only to do a good spring cleaning, it is to have a good glimpse at whom I am, at the same time succumbing to vermin, and hairiness everywhere: motionless in the hope of being deloused by another, and that other by another, and so on, until I don't know which loop is looped.

Delousing is a sincere desire to know: to know the other, this time, not only oneself, through the peeling of an effigy of great likeness (and which doesn't turn a hair so to speak): one can't imagine to which degree rummaging in the thickness of a primate's fleece brings about lessons on life: on ethics, morals, love, and the individual psychology and on our poor apes' metaphysics (delousing resembles playing *he loves me, he loves me not*, as well as decrypting a number code and flailing the wheat): how many times, as I was delousing, did I have the feeling to go searching not for a louse (or else an allegoric louse) but for the answer to the mystery of the universe and our presence in it.

Delousing is a psychoanalysis: it has almost everything to be exactly that, it pokes at intimacy, presupposes calm exchanges between patient and therapist, is concerned if not with psyche at least with scalp, which sometimes amounts to the same thing – and, anyway, it is renowned for doing a lot of good.

Delousing is an applied form of compassion: without for all that invoking God and his kindness raining on our sinners' heads, nor Jesus and his right cheek and his spit in the eye of a one-eyed man: compassion pure and simple, a straight line between subject A and subject B, followed by conclusive results: a beautiful exchange, the beginning of trade if trade was the consequence of pity and solidarity: on one side B rid of his parasite, on the other A, pleased with his cocktail snack.

Delousing is arithmetic, if a louse plus a louse plus another louse, plus another series of lice prompts the invention of numbers and addition in order to do the count, as would two, then three, finally n white pebbles on a sandy beach. I lack the time, but I would succeed in demonstrating how delousing, rather than the louse itself, comparable to a sign of punctuation, at the same time zero and one, stimulates mathematics as naturally as pollen stimulates bouts of sneezing (I would need time, and lax grammar, unless I make of my demonstration another delousing session: it would be for you, *sapiens sapiens*, to offer me your scalp and to learn the special language of grooming in order to understand me).

And delousing, to finish with, delousing is delousing itself, to make it simpler: the most obvious expression, for a monkey, of the desire to search, without necessarily expecting any gratification, or discovery, but to lose oneself in that search, to forget oneself while doing so, to find some respite in that selflessness – to take over a microcosm, find there a kind of welcoming, inhabit it minutely, and while trying to prove one is something more than the banana attached to the bunch attached to the tree, and something other than the louse, hoping for oneself another life than a sedate life: delousing oneself, delousing the other, spending one's time looking for imperceptible and eventually non-existent vermin the size of a pip, it is to never stop wanting to find fulfilment, instead of being contented with just being and existing as one sits on a stool. In the end, after an hour or so of that grooming, sorting out fleeces, discovering the unexpected tender pale pink skin of a new born under a thickness of wild fur, one comes to the conclusion that time hasn't been spent to capture a louse, but to free oneself of oneself. .

Chapter 38

THE ANIMAL TYPES

The afternoon drags on, according to the fiftieth version: one does not see the shadows stretching, as on the sandy beaches of melancholic novelists (autumnal), but it's all the same: the light is fading, dusk will soon mean darkness and backache and quickly (fifty-first version) the moment will come when McIntosh will have to replace the *soft half-light* with a *harsh light*, by turning on the ceiling lamp (a bulb or a neon). Still leaning on the mechanisms of the Remington, looking like he's inspecting the chassis of a 1908 Dion-Bouton, the typist carries on with his work, exhausting all in one: the combinations, his patience and his energy as adult ape fed on banana flesh (a parenchymatous tissue full of starch bearing the aroma of an acetate of isoamyl, that said once and for all): he types, he does it with his copyist's patience, monk or lawyer's clerk, but also, if one looks closer, the meticulousness of, how should I say?, a miniaturist at the moment he's covering an initial letter with golden powder, without sneezing – he no longer has that look of a mechanic, on the contrary, he displays a remarkable concentration, visible on his face, his coat, right to the tips of his hair, as if it too participated in the writing in its own way, by quivering: Percival no longer types randomly, he composes, he chooses, he proves to be judicious, he adopts parsimony and at each step (each key bashed and each letter) questions the relations between cause and consequence: a *t* doesn't come before an *o* for nothing, an *e* doesn't follow a *b* for no good reason, and all the letters lined on a page according to a certain order shake, as the Cabalists would way, shake discreetly our world.

This time there can't be any doubt — McIntosh himself, at the same time a witness and in charge, must take it into account, and in that purpose, must rub his eyes —: Percival the typist has just composed on half a page of blank paper, ten lines from *The Tempest*, signed William Shakespeare (according to the 1623 folio: *You taught me language, and my profit on't | Is, I know how to curse: the red-plague rid you [etc.]*): let's be clear now, he doesn't compose them randomly, but in cold blood, a cold blood which is also the felicity of the chaffinch as it dances on the strings of a lute.

After that, everything is moving faster (the fifty-second version): Percival, more skilful still, typing with his ten fingers, including the little one, selecting among all those letters the very best, gradually composes at his own leisure, very meticulously, Hamlet's monologue, several declamations belonging to Falstaff (from *The Merry Wives* and *Henry V*), a dialogue between Puck and Oberon — forging ahead, feeling exhilarated and ready to leap from the pages of books, he undertakes the writing of chapter 17 of the stories of the Baron de Crac by Gottfried Bürger *(Marvellous Travels on Water and Land: Campaigns and Comical Adventures of the Baron of Münchhausen)*, then abandons it for the third chapter of the *Gallant Ladies,* Brantôme-style *(Concerning the beauty of a fine leg, and the virtue the same doth possess)*; after that, still intoxicated, at least as much as a cyclist on a slope one spring morning, he composes a piece from La Fontaine (*Bertrand and Raton, etc...*) followed by an extract from Isaac Newton's *Principia*, then, for a change, a few pages from *Statistical Mechanics and Irreversibility*, penned by Emile Borel, which quite spontaneously gives him the opportunity to have before his very eyes, but written by himself this time, that immemorial story of monkeys who are given sufficient time to write on the typewriter, *the exact copy of the books of all nature and all languages kept in,* etc, etc.

He loses neither his energy not his theme; he loses none of his lucidity (his courage): according to the following version, Percival the typist warms up his machine, his ribbon turns with the speed of the straps: but this time, dropping Emile Borel, Isaac Newton or Falstaff, abandoning imitation to the indecisive and the inexperienced in order to give himself to pure creation, he improvises without weariness, in one hundred and twenty pages or so, 99 variations on the same canvas: the story of a chimpanzee and his Remington (on the edge of the 100th, he allows himself some rest, exhausted, famished, but above all proud of the mission accomplished, as a human being would be facing a heap of drafts). One can guess that from certain turns of phrase: a big slab of irony enters that feat: to write without any illusion 99 versions on the same theme, that is to play with accuracy, or lack of it regarding the text, seriousness, needless repetition, parody and open betrayal, to progressively move, without seeming to, from respecting the codes to dilettante subversion then to full-blown prank, is not only showing proof of his intelligence but demonstrating to what degree that device which ties a living animal to the keyboard of a typewriter is an absurdity: cruel and futile, and extravagant.

Chapter 39

THE ANIMAL SEVERELY CRITICISES HIS FELLOW CREATURE, THEN CONFORTS HIM

The version of the fifty-fourth fable drives home the point: Percival the chimpanzee, the descendant of Sultan through Semiramis, the worthy cousin of Sarah from the Woodruff, Premack & Knel's, worthy of Bandit, Belle and Bido (in 1973, at Menzl's), using five symbols painted on thick cardboard (*man, Percival, banana, yes, no, typewriting-machine*) explains to McIntosh the clinician that he is a real ass: to make an ape sit in front of a typewriter is the undeniable proof. Stoical, McIntosh doesn't seem to want to understand (for the very reason that he is an ass, or a little proud still, or because to refuse the judgement of his friend, especially because it is scathing, is one of the attributes of the human species). Percival regrets his words straight away (the thickness of the cards has nothing to do with this curt tone); he judges himself harsh, wild perhaps, descended from the trees without measuring his strength, finally unworthy of a human friendship: he would like to show his compassion before the end of the fifty-fourth fable: difficult however to comfort a friend with the only words available to him (*man, Percival, banana, yes, no, typewriting-machine*).

Chapter 40

THE ANIMAL FEELS ALONE

McIntosh too is bored to death: he gives his solitude a tone of languid agitation, that is, he thinks, the tone of lovers when the loved one is absent – he would like, if possible, to get rid of his white coat, his ball-point pens, his rake and his calculator, well everything that points to him being a lab assistant. Even if it means to be impatient, even if it means to wait by biting his nails, he would like to do it like a disappointed lover, not like a specialist in large numbers having had plenty of time to understand that Shakespeare's sonnets are not for tomorrow. Even if it means to be doomed to failure, he would like to fall in love, cry in hankies, write a name on a sheet of paper, weigh the pro and cons, measure his chances of happiness to the very last microgram almost fifty times a day, he would like to smarten himself up, find himself ugly, readjust his tie, search for hours for his elegance then get rid of it for fear of looking formal, adore his fiancée then wish her in hell, look with his last drop of energy for a single defect but a latent one that would free him from absolute love, and during that time, portray the sweetest girl in the world.

Pacing up and down brings McIntosh periodically level with the Remington – Percival does nothing more than persevere –: he can be seen leaning over and studying the latest draft under way, but instead of looking for preliminary drafts of *Love's Labour's Lost*, he takes a malicious almost discourteous pleasure in reading, in a series of *xpfrtkjsdf* and *çkghrtpqz*, the perfect expression for his melancholy.

Chapter 41

THE ANIMAL
COMPOSES AN ELEGY
FOLLOWED BY A PRAYER

If we are to believe the fifty-fifth version of the fable, Percival composes in a few pages of 500 words each, a theory (like the one he knows how to do now), on the solitude, old age and death of his lab assistant (perhaps a kind of elegiac prose); he would like to ward off ill-fortune, alas: to theorise McIntosh's death never made McIntosh immortal.

His theory goes along the lines of: perhaps you had pity on me, young assistant, you worried about my solitude a long time after you tied me to that typewriter while expecting feats of writing from me: came the time you felt like entertaining me, to steal me away from my solitary melancholy, with bananas, two then ten, and tree branches, and poles passing for tree branches, and toys in the shape of dolls, what you called soft toys – you expected to see me recreating a family of material and acrylic, you didn't imagine me satisfying my libido through masturbation. Solitude, if it exists, presupposes other remedies: you forgot the bananas and soft toys, and together we imagined a community of young ape typists, six then seven if you count me in, each with his or her own machine, in other words their instrument, in a riotous emulation of poets, harpsichord players, the atmosphere of a Dixieland Band and scriptorium (but a mischievous scriptorium) – and as we liked that version of the fable, for it entertained us a few days in a row, you took care to graft on it a chapter on love. Now I can tell you, McIntosh: my solitude is not so deep, it had its recreations, some company, love, the true comradeship between monkeys like the conversation of drinkers above the banqueting table, and the more refined complicity of the well-read; you can see me replete, surrounded by friends, serene with the idea that a group of two hundred chimpanzees are waiting for me somewhere, in Borneo or its surroundings, and will shake the trees to welcome me the day I will choose to leave here – but you, McIntosh, you: during that time, busy bringing me bananas and soft toys, comrades and love tokens, what did you do about your solitude? Did you lean over it if only for one minute? Did you measure its breadth? And do you know how many solitudes it is relying on? You measured the sociability of a young ape with exact criteria without noticing the silence that was gathering around you – in reality, if I was not here to make the keys of that machine jingle, the silence would now be complete (it would have been from the start), you would have faced the whiteness of the walls: because you are alone, and that no tribe of apes is waiting for you while shaking the tree branches. It makes me wonder if all that, that device of a Remington, of the lucky chance born of large numbers, of combinations, of animal behaviour and especially of the capture of an ape trained to play the polygraphs, all of that hasn't been worked out to help you find yourself a friend, a young chimpanzee for lack of anything better, him and his siblings fleas and lice – find yourself a friend and confide in him, one day on two, sometimes your joys, sometimes your sorrows. And I also wonder, now that I have become more skilful by bashing on those fifty keys, I wonder if your solitude as scholar gardener living apart in a remote corner of the zoo is not just a greater solitude, in a way heavier, that of the human species. I sometimes guess, in the way you turn round and round from one side of this room to the next, open the empty letterbox, hear in there the echo of your voice alone, and look to me in vain for a good pal with whom to play the decider at Scrabble, to what degree you, the most sapiens of all sapiens, suffer to find yourself alone – as if your solitude was a trial that the other primates were excluded from.

Your solitude is discreet; you don't howl in a vast empty space representing the infinity of the universe; you don't spend your time kicking a stone and cursing the fate that made you a being living on the edge of a galaxy, endowed with a conscience, capable of articulating the words *solitude* and *death*, capable also of considering their existence without having the slightest idea of their nature. You cultivate orchids, you cut flies in four, you compare two numbers as you compare two pear pips, you consider God and gravity, you measure the time elapsed and that which you have left to live, you capture herds, you could even desperately try to instil in macaques a language made of three or two signs, *yes, no, perhaps*, and all of that makes you singular, all of that makes you the intelligent type, too intelligent, talkative, escorted by his books, alone on his raft about to take on water while the whole crowd of the chosen ones sailed away on a boat. You wonder if having been able to apprehend the universe, having wanted to apprehend it, at least having laid down the necessary gestures, having sprung from the earth and without getting rid of your primate's passions, having applied your reason to it, all of that doesn't cost you today's solitude (it doesn't weight on you, it doesn't make you suffer, it is what you pretend anyway, it makes you think [tell me, is there something in this world that doesn't make you think? What about a turbot served with mayonnaise? A sneeze at the moment of sneezing?]).

Chapter 42

THE ANIMAL
DRESSES UP
AS AN ANIMAL

Several versions of the fable choose tragic endings, they don't hide any dark undertone in order to give some substance to tales judged too light in the eyes of others: the more death there is, the more admirable are the tales: so the funny story of an ape sitting in front of his keyboard, we may as well say a hen with its penknife, reaches the sublime summits of Shakespearean drama, while it was considered a three line joke written on a toffee wrapper. In one of those versions, Percival ends up dying, it's natural, old age added to overwork: in the arms of Samuel McIntosh he jumps, gasps, hiccups, raises his eyes, looks for the last time at earthly things, sneezes and dies, or dies and sneezes, after which McIntosh attends to the rise of his soul (his spirit), through his half-open chops (then: the open window, the sea breeze, west, north-west).

It is the fifty-sixth version of the fable: dead on the job, dead after having pressed the last key of the last letter, one among others, Percival the chimpanzee shrunk into a corner of the room, there where quite recently, recently, piles of paper were rising high as a teenage baboon standing on its two legs. He is not just dead: one has the feeling he signifies death, shrivelled that way: fixed stare and dry eyes, looking like a pair of figs, jaw half-open and tongue poking out, slightly to the side, going from pink to black – his hair dull, he will smell rancid soon.

Before the rancid smells, way before them, when death is still fresh, at least as much as a day-fresh egg, McIntosh the lab assistant, according to

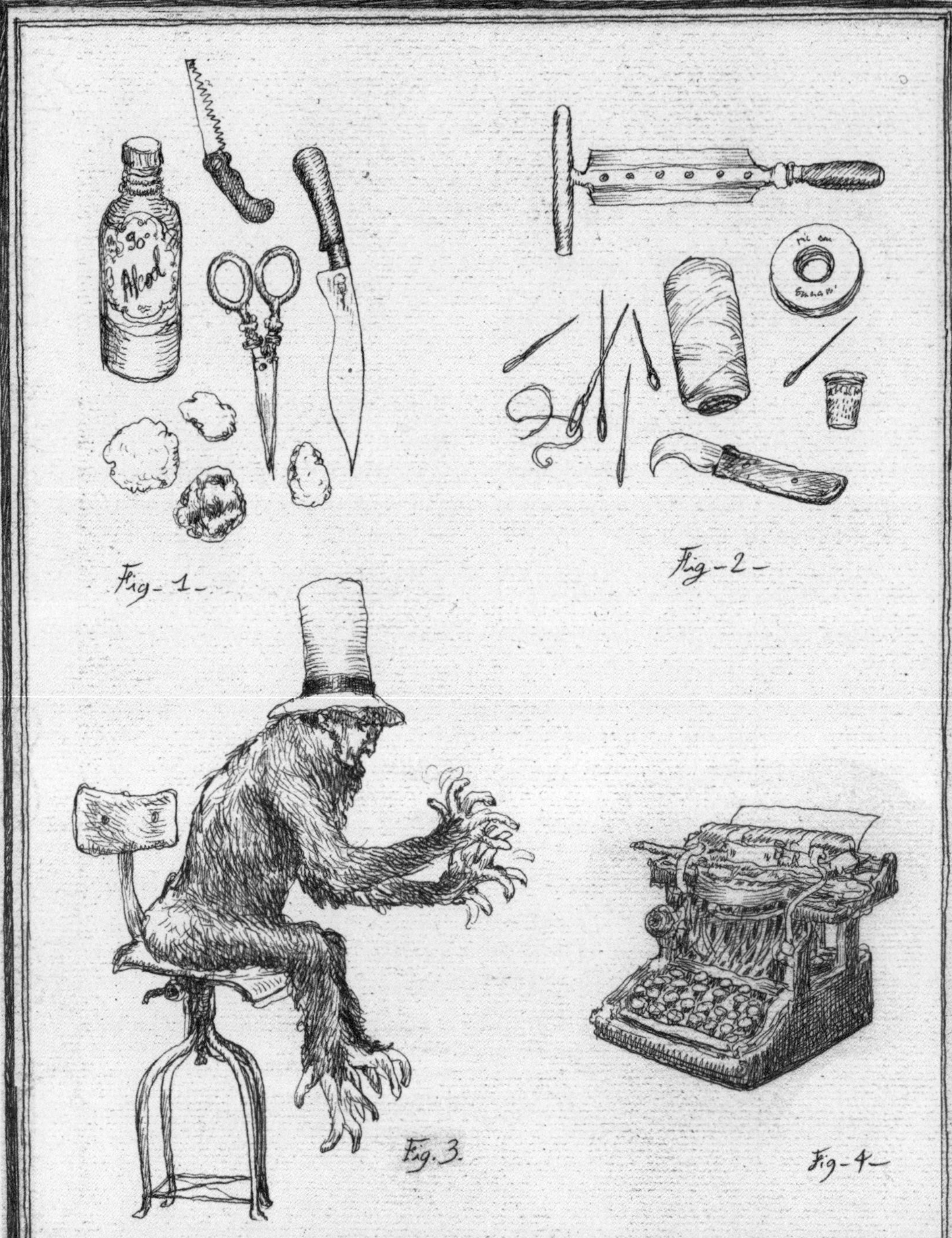

90° Alcool
Fig - 1 -
Fig - 2 -
Fig. 3.
Fig - 4 -

the fifty-sixth version, gathers what he knows about taxidermy: he recovers some alcohol and scalpels from the anatomy department, as well as bags of cotton wool. He is seen skinning his old friend (he can't come to terms with death flouting his experiment), separating hide from remains, no longer aware if Percival, his identity, his essence is more present in the fur than in the naked flesh — after that he is seen cleaning, scraping, soaking, scenting, sowing, re-sowing, undertaking the great making. In the next chapter, he comes up, unrecognisable, covered with that fur, except for his head: his toes find it slightly difficult to adapt to the suppleness of the fingers, but they do the best they can, each in its own way, rediscovering at each step the art of being prehensile — and for each hair, it is almost the same stakes and same trials (how to accept the idea of being sensitive, of being for oneself and for the ape the antenna of resentment, how to stand on end, or get soft in order to express fear or desire to seduce, and finally how to face the permanent responsibility of signifying from dawn to dusk at least as much as a man's face).

The fifty-sixth fable is premonitory: it has McIntosh walking to his chair in his costume, leaning over the Remington, clenching his teeth, enduring those itches that remind him of his childhood woollies, when he had to recycle his big brother's jumper and at the same time engage in the adoption of its resident moths. He is sweating: perspiration will perhaps be the mortar that connects his man's skin, in other words, his baby skin, to that old ape's rind — he does not roll up his sleeves, but valiantly takes it up from where Percival had failed.

Chapter 43

THE ANIMAL
SHARES
A GLASS OF ALCOHOL
WITH HIS FELLOW CREATURE

According to the fifty-seventh to sixty-second versions, it's dusk, soon it will be time for a rest (neither the typist ape, nor the Remington being inexhaustible):it's time to favour conviviality in the form of a pause around a glass of alcohol and a few peanuts, also from Indonesia – in the circumstance, a cup of dry white Martini in which an olive floats, over-meaningful: the idea is to celebrate that first day of work. Until now, Samuel McIntosh has never been inclined towards drunkenness, he is never spotted on the lowest floor of an inn knocking back brandies in quick succession: rather, he takes little sips, he takes delight, he sees it coming from afar: and if what he sees coming is intoxication, a good old drunkenness, it has the merit of being palliative, inviting to go by degrees from realism to a fantasy made of hypotheses, then to absurdity, followed by sleep after the absurd, as one talks about a cigarette after love-making. Under Borneo's foliage, Percival, surrounded by his relatives (patriarchs, who knew everything there was to know about the fermentation of extracts of ripe fruits), he managed to learn about alcohol by imitating his fellow apes, the same way he dipped a stick (which type of stick, a divining rod?) into the nest of termites in order to reach the sweets – but it was a tiny intoxication, barely perceptible, a discretion on the scale of 1 to 1,000: taking that scale into account, the equivalent of a flea on the back of an African elephant, pink on grey, minute though distinct. There, under the branches, the young ape felt unsteady on his feet, he who was never familiar with the sea, nor the waves, nor nautical art, nor sailors' songs, only the lullabies of his childhood accompanied by the movement of the palm leaves.

A second, then a third, still white, ivory Martini with its olive: it is for McIntosh and his colleague the opportunity to assess, as one says, that first day's experience, by going through the drafts, trying to find at least one word correctly spelt, even a brief word, accepted by the dictionary, lost in the middle of a line of *lxsrdgpltfh* (but in all honesty — for all science presupposes procedures, observations, reports, sometimes sterilised blades, but above all scruples: the scruples of saints in white coats and with pencils nicely sharpened — in all honesty McIntosh refuses to read in each apparition of the capital I the expression, in Shakespearean English, of a conscious, articulated, demanding and already poetic, in other words, musical *I*). They sip, both of them, they leaf through the sheets, they share green olives, talk about the chance that they try to portray, to dismember as one would take apart a mosaic fragment by fragment — with the third glass they feel the hour of congratulations and fraternity coming, the hour when one has to give oneself to the physical, chemical and mechanical phenomenon of sympathy: with blurred eyes, to discover in one another twenty, thirty, a thousand affinities, and as many mutual interests, convictions, emotions, passions shared between old primate brothers. At the fourth glass, Samuel McIntosh and Percival are at the point when they establish, without either paper or pen the list of shared characteristics that bring man and ape together on the same branch: reason, gaze, expression of the face, desire to laugh, standing position, the thumb opposable to the other four fingers, the auricle, the brain hippocampus, lips, curiosity, the ribs of adolescence, the awareness of death, the desire to seduce, the need for love, the mating display, crisis through melancholy, waking up on the wrong side of the bed so to speak, desire and hope, and various other aptitudes that are lost here in the haze of alcohol.

At the fifth glass, the two colleagues, rather somewhat tenderized now (how should I say?, penetrable, almost porous), evoke humanity compared to animality, in other words mankind and what is particular to man, a kind of precious ornament, rare, wrongly identified, and fleeing, after which everyone has started to run, Aristotle in the lead, but which will always escape, like a marble on a slope heading towards inaccessible chasms (or inaccessible recesses).

At the sixth, they are creating a bilingual dictionary McIntosh/Percival – Percival/McIntosh, enriched with examples, conjugations, phonetics and beautiful abbreviations which are the ornaments of linguistics – at the seventh glass, Martini has to be replaced by Burgundy wine, which should (in McIntosh's words, the fifty-eighth version of the fable) smooth the rough edges of inebriation.

A little while later (one stopped counting glasses and bottles: algebraic scruples have their limits too), in the chapters of the fifty-ninth and sixtieth versions of the fable McIntosh confides in his friend his childhood memories, in fragments, and in no particular order (solitude and gregariousness, awkwardness and precocious virtuosity, dreams and dreams interrupted, chicken pox and super human strength, blindness and second sightedness are mentioned; some details are also disclosed that are visible to the naked eye only). In the chapters of the sixty-first and sixty-second versions, it is the opposite: Percival confides his childhood to his assistant, attentive doctor, big brother and old pal (primary forests are brought up as well as arboricultural equilibrium, downpours and rivers, collective enthusiasms – for the rest, it is the same combination of solitude and gregariousness, awkwardness and virtuosity, to which Percival adds exacerbated shyness and daredevil boldness).

Chapter 44

THE ANIMAL
DEFENDS THE SUBTLETY
OF HIS EMOTIONS

The sixty-third version waits for the moment when intoxication reaches one of its highest degrees to make Percival talk at great length along this line:

Although I'm only a chimp, from the order of chimpanzees, family and class of chimpanzees, I experience complex feelings: hunger and thirst are primary colours, I leave them far behind; my experience, my sensitivity (hypersensitivity) as young ape has been leading me for a long time now to handle the most elegant nuances, much more elegant — as I leave love, anger, pride, humiliation to macaques less gifted than I am, happy as they are to manipulate crude emotions, like coconuts used for axioms and intuition. In order to give a written form to my exquisite and fraught emotions, I should learn the alphabet, the order and disorder of the alphabet, then the grammar, and read a whole repertoire dedicated to melancholy (or composed by melancholic authors). Believe me, my feelings are a refinement of psychology, in which mixed motifs are barely perceptible except perhaps for some witnesses, themselves super sensitive, aware for a long time of the slightest movement, the faint lights and the shadows resembling those lights. All around me, other great apes compose crude associations: thirst + jealousy, or libido + terror; the cleverest combine three emotions in order to have three-of-a-kind, like desire + humility + stubbornness. As far as I'm concerned, alone on my branch, I have to make much more ambitious bouquets of a hundred and thousand flowers, like that association of regret + patience + pride +

humility + boldness + shame + daydreaming + terror + memory + recognition + desire to seduce + discretion + kindness + curtness + amazement + lassitude + despair + irony + vague resentment with no object + joy of living while swinging within reach of a bunch of bananas. To narrate a single emotion born after all the others, I would need enough paper, and for that paper enough trees, in other words to sacrifice Borneo's entire forest, where I was born, where I would like to take shelter one of these days.

Chapter 45

THE ANIMAL
TALKS ABOUT HUMANITY

In the sixty-fourth version the alcoholic drinks are identical, but the speech on feelings is replaced by a discourse on humanity:

There are always obstacles to clear: first to dip the sweet potato in the water, then show compassion, then bury the dead, then respect the rules of grammar – I will reach the ultimate state of humanity, I know that, on the day I will succeed in calling into question *your* humanity, my dear lab assistant: I would find a beautiful intelligence, that's for sure, skill, a capacity for adaptation, perhaps the beginning of a sensitivity, three pennies worth of memories, and a clever tongue, but humanity, well, well, let's not exaggerate – (etc.)

Chapter 46

THE ANIMAL
TALKS ABOUT HIS SELF
AND ABOUT HIMSELF

It's the sixty-fifth version's turn to serve the same bottles, but to replace the discourse on humanity with an improvisation on the self:

I am myself, I am nothing else, nor anyone else, I am not in any case my closest neighbour, nor my whole neighbourhood, male and female included, nor the fruit that I squeeze in my hands in order to extract its juice according to its nature, and prove myself superior to the plant. The most difficult is to go and find a colleague, let's say a chimpanzee, pan-troglodyte, with a nice face, rather clever if possible, with a sparkle of intelligence in his eyes, which will please the zoologists — find that colleague, wake him from his nap, which would mean tear him from his primate's future (not only his past), shake off his fleas, mark with him the slight difference between monkey's trade and conversation between consenting adults. Once convinced I am facing a bright primate coming out of his haze, it's essential that I look him straight in the eyes, to search those eyes for a trace of intelligence through which I could worm my way in (there's something sensual about that, perhaps intrusive too), to wait for the right moment, the sparse right moment in Borneo's forest on unstable branches — and once sure of myself, of my deed, to share my deepest thought with my partner: a certainty, the certainty to be myself, nobody else, not that big hairy ape fond of termites nor that thin capuchin monkey looking like a coconut pierced with three nostrils. It's my partner's turn to look at me, intensely, or let's say with all the

intensity available according to the circumstances – at that instant only,
I understand (which is not a discovery) that the certainty of being myself
depends for ever on the certainty of the other to be other, in other words
to be a self, also subjected to the conviction of a neighbour, and so on, for
lack of what, instead of a certainty, remains the intuition comparable to
hunger or thirst, or in the mating season, to the desire to flirt.

Chapter 47

THE ANIMAL
EVOKES
HIS MATINGS

The sixty-sixth version opts for the confidence genre (conforms undoubtedly to the drunkard's genre):

How did I manage to convince Rebecca, my Rebecca, my gorgeous female ape with her soft hair, almost auburn (and her mother-of-pearl skin, there where the hair is sparse, to give the lover a delicious impression of immodesty [perhaps the offering, perhaps the least she can do]) – how did I convince her to have done with copulation in order to give herself over to love-making? Difficult to say: it was a Thursday afternoon, on or under a branch, my ape's memory is fallible, altered by emotions as it has probably been by hard blows. Rebecca and I did accomplish courageous efforts, aware of the harmony between things, especially the harmony of our passion with the laws of nature; our sex responded to our desire (or should I say: *were quick to respond*?); we had aims that were real and precise, a bit of fantasy in fatality, but, to be honest, more tenacity or anxiety about pulling through with no harm than real virtuosity – and I'm not even talking about climaxing here. At which moment, at which minute did Rebecca let herself be convinced by my arguments that were higgledy-piggledy words of love, passionate discourse, awkward caresses and sighs of consternation? I couldn't say that either, all the more for my delightful lover, instead of letting herself be convinced, could as easily have pretended, for my male satisfaction, perfectly aware that she was offering to her lover the most beautiful, the easiest of gratification: to succumb to his reasonings at the same time as she was to his weight and following his thrusts. For all that: we succeeded, I think, at least we were on the point of succeeding: on the point of reversing our ape destiny, once and for all, of exorcising fornication so as to embark as lovers and primates on the path to eroticism – we would have succeeded for good, with a moving panache, exhaustion and cries of the victors if, at the same time, I don't know which gesture among all those we had to accomplish had us losing our balance, the fragile but precious balance with which (despite or thanks to which) we were accomplishing on that day our mating on the branch. What follows is easy to guess: the fall, the pain, the humiliation, the rage, and, instead of an orgasm, two unrelated little jerks, in the high grass, and too much despair and bumps to still have the strength to find in that fall the essence of eroticism – since then I hang on to my old hypotheses, while Rebecca hangs onto her new lover's arms.

Chapter 48

THE ANIMAL DREAMS OF A VEGETAL LIFE

Finally, according to the sixty-seventh to seventy-fourth versions, the alcoholic drinks, all more or less fruity, inspire digressions on vegetal life:

And why not a vegetative life, to put an end once and for all to those heartbreaks – to no longer have to choose between animal existence and human destiny? To rid oneself of those anxieties of great ape hesitating between *sapiens sapiens* and pan-troglodyte, Cartesian meditation and delousing ceremony, artistic melancholy and crude good-nature of monkey knocked senseless by his determinism and by the fall of a cousin coming from the branch above? (We are now in the middle of the night, in the haze of alcohol, among the remains of nibbles, mulled wine, punch and lemon slices; the eyes are blurred but the friendship sincere: according to the sixty-seventh version of the fable, Percival and McIntosh reach that stage of inebriation when every brotherhood is conceivable, even possible: including the friendship of an octopus and an orange pip). To envy plants (the big trees, the ferns, the euphorbias, the eucalyptus, everything that comes out and turns green), resemble them, push the analogy and mimicry beyond the limits usually accepted, would be indeed the opportunity to put a term to those worries of hominoid primate, always on the point of taking himself for a man, or monkeying about. No, a vegetative life does not come down to the prostration of an idiot having spent a hundred years on a chair, slobber serving as spring sap in the corner of his lips and corns as roots; vegetative life can be

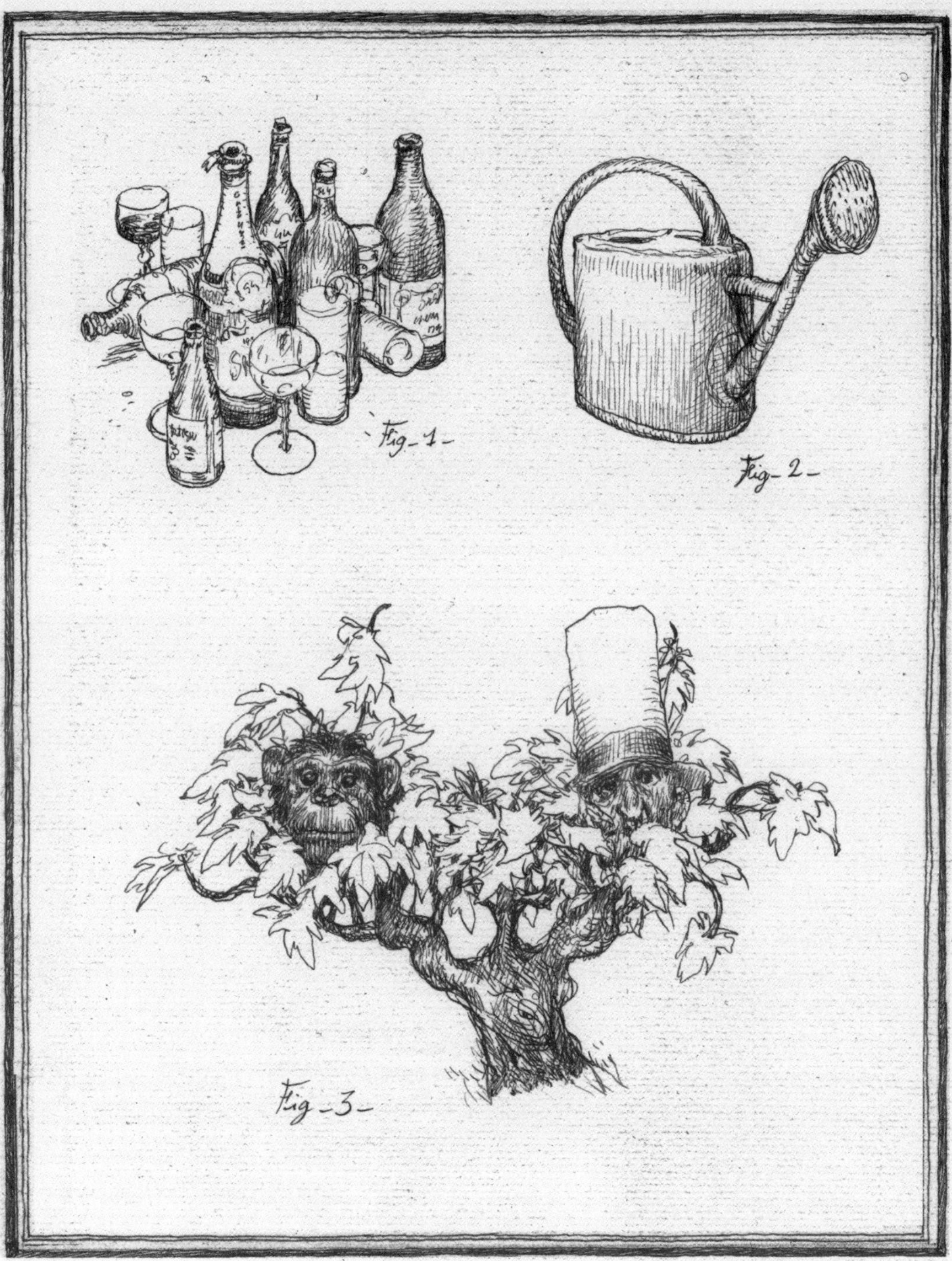

- Fig - 1 -
- Fig - 2 -
- Fig - 3 -

dynamic, impulsive, enthusiastic, boisterous, ruffled, unbearable; stillness is ascribed to the vegetable kingdom so that one can talk about it better, or hack into it (or lie on it, if it's the grass of a clearing, for example, a compromise between velvet and matting). A vegetal life would be for Percival and McIntosh taken together (two drunk heads, one vine foot), to lead a serene existence without the shaking of our nerves, a life unfolded in space as in time: to sum it up, an existence made of one single huge opening out, in corolla or fan-shaped, serving as biography, adventure, teenage crisis, formative novel, good and bad fortune, maturity, long journeys at sea, erotic escapades, professional ambitions, yawning, nap, headlong flight, mating display, sunbathing and gastronomy, and finally meditation.

And that's what Percival, still soaked in alcohol (as much as a fruit, the sixty-ninth version specifies, a crystallised fruit as Christmas and its cakes and puddings approaches), adds in McIntosh's ear, merry, dancing around, I mean losing his footing, also hit by the grape harvest, busy stretching between his drunken self and a hypothetical future lucid self (sobered up, confident), an allegoric thread on which he would play the tightrope walker, at the same time concerned about his balance and on the verge of breaking his neck – here is what he adds: to live like a maple tree, or like a thousand maple trees, or a whole maple plantation would allow the two of us to also exorcise the demons of solitude; when one exists like a vegetable the distinction between *alone isolated from all* and *surrounded by a million similar fellows* become much more vague; branching out ad infinitum, growing old from division to division to give birth to another self next to oneself like a green leaf next to the same green leaf, is ideal to stave off one's boredom, to feel surrounded, hard luck if what surrounds us is the core which constitutes us and the fabric of our appearance – it gives birth to those suckers to talk to, and deliver us from a certain fragility.

And then and then (according to the seventieth version: Percival is sitting astride an oak barrel, busy symbolising the animal dionysism saturating the human dionysism – his tongue feels all furry, he argues furrily): isn't branching out an agreeable way of life? I mean, to pass the time, grow in age and size, become more refined, make oneself more complex, become more hairy, an impenetrable but delicate openwork, occupy the space while emptying one's head, let the light pass through oneself and offer to the squirrels all sorts of fulcrums? What would you say if, from now on, watered with brandy, we decided to blossom while dividing at each of our intersections, instead of simply getting fat or becoming callous, and make several series of folds? (Man and ape have that in common, you know: they become wrinkled with age, not for the sheer fun of trapping the dust from outside, but to increase sensibly their surface, and offer it to rays of light with the ingenuousness and generosity of a houseplant.) From division to division, from branch to branch, if only you knew to which extent one becomes more refined, so pointed at the tip, imperceptible and diaphanous, almost poetic: one gets reduced without ever wanting to end for good – and then you should know that we would finally have the opportunity to cross paths.

Our distinctions are pointless (according to the seventy-first version), this time it's McIntosh's turn to play the feed: he blows in a stemmed glass and searches the bottomless bottom of a bottle for the eye he thinks he lost): a single graft would be sufficient to join us, and forget every grammatical difference (physical, material) between you and me, man and animal: a few days would be enough to see your hair running over my arm. I promise you, comrade (and according to the 71(b) version, McIntosh raises a finger almost vertically more or less towards the sky): leading our vegetative life would enable us to finally do without our so cumbersome self, yours and mine: that self one has to pamper, feed, dress and fuss over, constantly justify, revive, inflate fully, or, on the opposite, bring down to fairer proportions (vanity being an illness of scale).

And have you thought about bursting into blossom? Blossoming without being ill? Blossoming without having to go through a fever, blossoming without waiting for the eruptions of adolescence, blossoming each month of May for the sheer enjoyment of being pale pink, signifying spring, charming at little cost, carrying out natural cycles and sowing seeds in public, which would give us discourses on the relativity of the sense of modesty.

And what about bearing fruits, growing heavy, bending – *bending*: that's what we said in those cases – under one's own abundance, being wasteful, being generous, having some of those bulges, nurturing a cult for glucose and fresh flesh, promising delights so simple, Arcadian, and keeping one's promises and after that, let the fruit drop, all the fruits, one by one, learning to part with a piece of oneself, drawing from that lessons on detachment, if not from putrefaction, another form of joy of living.

To live stupidly like a man or a chimpanzee has its advantages, certainly, undeniably (that's what Percival declares to McIntosh, according to the seventy-second version: the one that unfolds beneath high ceilings, in panellings, the whiteness of the laboratory replaced by the amber of a library): we both have nimble fingers, a flexible tongue, enough to encourage us to sing and have sex; our nerve endings are sometimes the sources of pleasure, we have locomotion and a tiny bit of intelligence, one doesn't happen without the other; as an animal, we have hobbies, a few gifts, prerogatives, like being able to savour (the banana, the elegiac style), to be emancipated, to play cat and mouse without being either cat or mouse; to succumb to reproduction does not mean for you or me to pollinate like mad, unconsciously, in April wind: out of the question to multiply without feeling: we have that incredible luck to be sexed and concupiscent at the same time, and to be able to convert fatality into pleasure. That's all fine, certainly, undeniably: but think for a second about the advantages offered to the plant: to be solar, essentially solar, to live in languor, exposing oneself to the day, no longer to have to chew on old rubbery turnips or the flesh of the cow, or black pudding while we are at it, but to absorb the energy we lack in the shape (fluid, evanescent, spiritual) of light: that would be the first step towards angelism, wouldn't it? And we would accept once and for all the geranium as the missing link between animal and seraph.

And what about the beautiful, the enviable longevity? Your device of chair, typewriter, complete works and chance slowly happening presupposes immortality, which is not suited to animal, man or ape, used to short terms, in reality pathetic: your experiment would have been more successful if you had replaced the chimpanzee with a baobab, for example, an indefatigable baobab which only lacks loose fingers. Can you imagine, you and me, chlorophyllous, two hundred years old, still green, venerable, serene, far above our daily business, very high at the top, with a view over a panorama stretching from North to South, East to West, capable still of bearing fruits once a year, not so bad, but having become tough enough to let some people taking a stroll, very small those human brothers, scratch their names on our bark: our skin in its thickness would have the hospitality of a parchment.

To become vegetative in order to have done with heartbreaks: a spruce has never been seen crying while reciting Romeo, or Werther, and jumping from a sloping forest of tall trees to put an end to a life of torments and ungrateful fiancées: neither the rhododendron nor the magnolia are familiar with ungrateful fiancées; there is no cruel passions, neither scenes of jealousy, nor of long waits and sad celibacy: the tree is tree, it can live without summer love or little flirtings, it could be a way for us to heal, as one says, the wounds of lovers turned away. There is no voluptuousness, there is no harem (at least if one believes in appearances), nothing but the serenity of a trunk, and an extreme slowness. But vegetative life perhaps conceals a sensuality we have no idea of (neither

I, big oaf living in the forest, nor you, bright genius with no future): a vegetative sensuality, deeper still, more inventive, surprising, vertiginous in the mating season, sweet and sour, permanent also, but diluted, deliciously vague, unfamiliar with any idea of successful outcome.

We would end up confusing life and death, by the sheer act of pretending to be trees, and becoming trees: death itself, dragged in the general confusion, would grant us a royal peace, a hypothetical ape peace, of a character from a fairy tale and thousand year-old forest: we would have eternity in front of us, for good this time: all the time needed to exhaust the combinations, those we are still missing and that are left for us to discover.

Our head would be far from our feet, we would have the elegance of poles, we would be green and pink at the same time, we would bend to wind and seasons, we would be mute, delightfully mute, there wouldn't be in us, nor around us, the obsession of the message — besieged by the deaf and blind, we would no longer care about signifying at all times, we would access a world devoid of misunderstandings; we would be slow and supple, both of us, we would have strange symmetries, we would resemble each other even more, we would act without always worry about acting, but the little gestures we would have would seem orchestrated, in harmony with one another; we would be discreet, an intrusive discretion: a very new instinct of plant would allow us to demonstrate the equivalence of humility and the vastest ambition; we would let time pass on us with such a hospitality, such a vegetal phlegm that we would end up representing that time and the future: the rest of the animal kingdom living in the duration that we will have become.

Chapter 49

THE ANIMAL
TAKES ROOT
AND BLOSSOMS

According to the chapters of the seventy-fifth version of the fable, Percival the chimpanzee and his lab assistant McIntosh don't just evoke a destiny of liana and tree, inspired by alcohol (which has the tendency to give limbs and ambitions disproportionate length): a notch above in the hierarchy of inebriation, they decide to act and, if we are to believe a pen and ink illustration, delicately hand-made, both take root, grow taller, divide up, create branching followed by more branching, go through the open window to make room for all that extension – outside, it is a summer night, it is definitely more in keeping with those vegetal exuberances, Percival and McIntosh venture there (creep like ivy, or wind through like wisteria), from the first floor to the ground floor, then the terrace, followed by the garden, the gravelled paths and, gradually, but at the speed of a grass snake, they spread across the whole surface of the zoo: they occupy it, bedeck it, cover it and survey it, all of that at the same time: by the sheer act of settling there, by night, they would end up usurping it, becoming the garden in place of the actual garden, hoping to be comfortable enough, in spite of the straw, thistle and thorns, to make a bed for the visitors: the mammals.

Chapter 50

THE ANIMAL REMINDS US OF THE BANKS OF THE NILE

Versions seventy-six to seventy-eight also want to take very seriously the leads opened by McIntosh and his ape Percival under the influence of the Bloody Mary: the vegetative life doesn't act as a whim but as a reality (one shouldn't underestimate the effects of alcohol, even less its persuasive force: under its authority, hypotheses remain convincing as hypotheses, and have no need for anything else to happen – understand by that, happen for real). If we are to believe the seventy-eighth version, for example, Percival really buries himself, less like a stationary ape than like the frail seedling of a papyrus: starry and gracious, absorbent, somewhat decorative, especially in that universe of the whitewashed hall, and exotic if it reminds us of the banks of the Nile, such as we imagine them.

Chapter 51

THE ANIMAL
MAKES
PHOTOSYNTHESIS

Version seventy-nine witnesses McIntosh turning green too and, in order to live, leaving it to the process of photosynthesis, and consequently getting closer to daylight, on the side closest to the window: not by walking, but by stretching, like any philodendron would do in his place.

Chapter 52

THE ANIMAL
TURNS
TOWARDS THE SUN

Still travelling along that vegetative track, version eighty shows Percival and his master McIntosh, still very hominoid in their appearance, big primates with no tails, but with a certain vegetal something in the way they turn: sensitive to the luminous spectrum, they adopt poses of heliotropes.

Chapter 53

THE ANIMAL
TAKES ROOT BUT CREEPS, GOES OVER, MAKES BRANCHES, INVADES AND BLOSSOMS AT EACH OF HIS TIPS

Versions eighty-one, eighty-two, eighty-three and eighty-four also choose to offer those two characters destinies of chlorophyll plants, but without renouncing for all that the adventures, journeys, movements that make the best serials (Rocambole, for example, hardly here, already elsewhere – and let's not even mention Baron Munchausen). As creepers from the ivy family, Percival and McIntosh cover kilometres that are worth Michel Strogoff's versts and Captain Nemo's leagues: having started from the pavilion concealed under the leaves at the bottom of an ornamental garden, they go over the windows and walls, cover street after street from the town centre to the barely less urban outskirts, and from there to the edge of the countryside, the assortment of brambles and rubbish heaps, and from there even further beyond industrial zones, above barriers decorated with beautiful adverts, towards the forest, towards the forest for good, or let's say towards the woods: the beech trees, the oaks, the aspens and a few country cops. Fable number eighty-five prolongs those journeys as far as England to the North, passing under the Channel, to Germany right across to the old East, forcing each character to live at the extremity of his two branchings, two series of adventures, no longer knowing which way to turn: in England stories of lawn, rain, peat bogs, gardens, haha, lords, mistresses, a little girl running after a white rabbit — in Germany, tales of black forest, pine trees, combes, up and down the hills, storms, brown potato fields towards Pomerania and an officer from the empire sailing above the trees astride a canon ball.

Chapter 54

THE ANIMAL
DIVIDES INTO TWELVE

According to version eighty-six, Percival, still chimpanzee, divides through cuttings (it presupposes a competent gardener and a credible narrator – credible as a story teller): twelve chapters make him lead, at the same time, twelve adventurous existences in twelve places where the cuttings had taken root: in Kyoto, a love story; in Baghdad, an incredible story; in Benares, a story of destiny; in Istanbul, a spy story; in Seville, a story of nuns; in Naples, a crime story; in Edinburgh, a ghost story; in Vienna, a story of bad luck; in Winnipeg, another love story; in New York, a money story; in Buenos Aires, a family saga; in Alexandria, a porn fantasy.

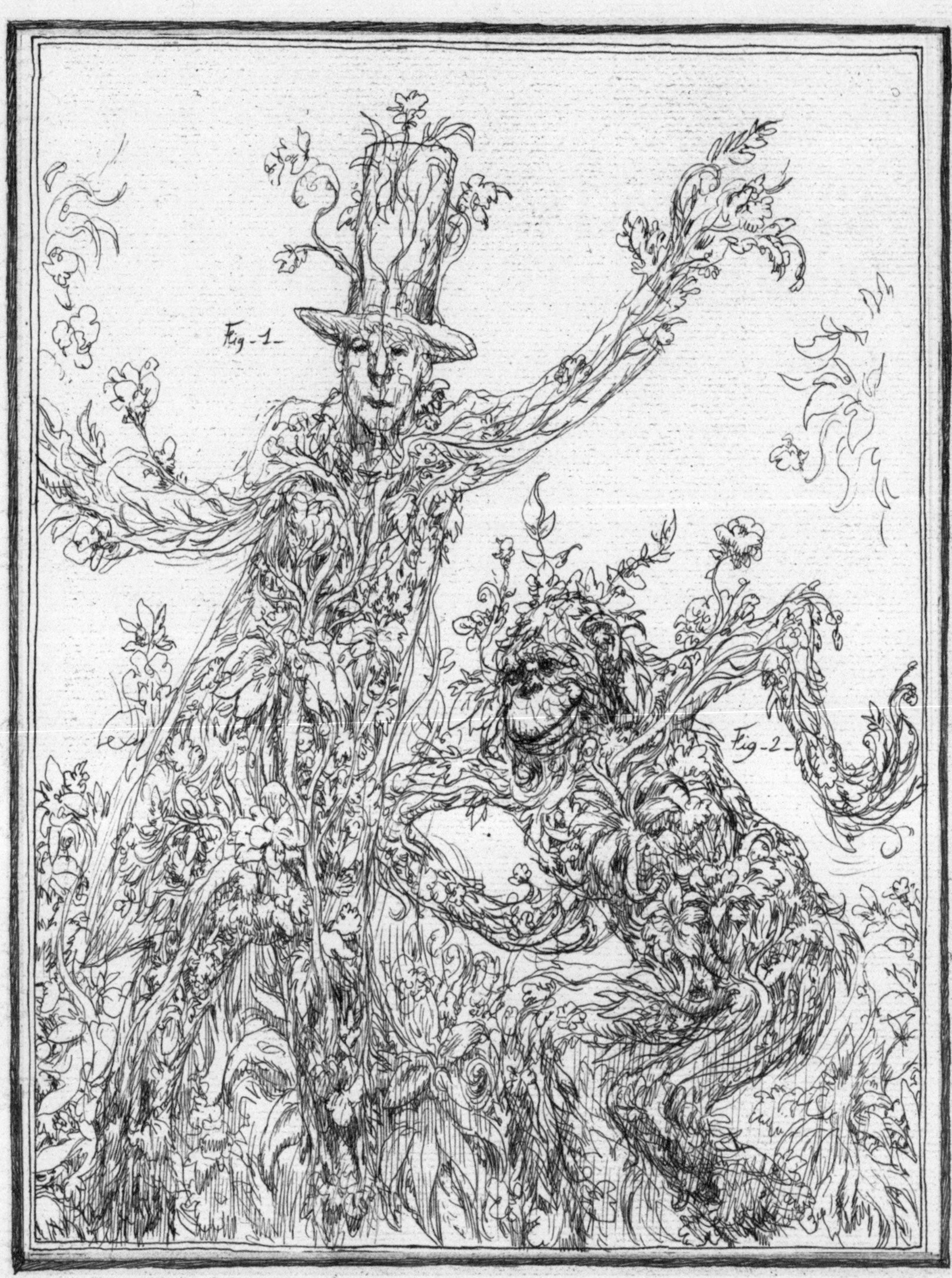
Fig. 1.
Fig. 2.

Chapter 55

THE ANIMAL
BECOMES DEXTROROTATORY

Put more simply, in the eighty-seventh version, Percival, a Japanese wisteria, and McIntosh, a Chinese wisteria, intertwine: one is dextrorotatory, the other levogyrous (both drunk).

Chapter 56

THE ANIMAL
LETS HIS BRANCHES HANG

Following the eighty-eighth version, Percival, having become a weeping willow, lets his branches hang over the keyboard of the Remington (his extremities are those of a tree *and* those of a typist: they are fine) as if he remembered his duty and invited the narrator to return to the story.

Chapter 57

THE ANIMAL
RETURNS TO THE STORY

In reality, the eighty-ninth version is a way to return to the fundamental, the most elementary, and that as far as the dénouement (one would think one was reading a manuscript found beneath fine sand, asleep for two thousand years, now uncovered and authentic as nibbled at by worms): a typist, seated before the keyboard of a Remington attempts to write at random all 22 scenes of *As You Like It* – during that time, the lab assistant dozes.

Everything is identical, except for this little bit: this time, McIntosh plays the typist and Percival the lab assistant: young chimpanzee pantroglodyte working for science while stroking his hair until it shines. The following version (the ninetieth) presents the advantage of conforming to the idea one has about the day after a piss-up: one sees Percival, prompter to recover from his hangover, waking up McIntosh (whose pasty face presents various nuances of whites and greens), shaking him, offering him at the same time the effervescence and the redemption (an aspirin), bringing him back to life, showing him daylight and the late hour in the afternoon, dragging him by the shoulder, and, making the most of his weakness, leading him to the desk, making him sit in front of a keyboard and inviting him, mischievously, sweetly, to type at random, without giving it a thought (*one is never served as well as by oneself*).

Chapter 58

THE ANIMAL SUBJUGATES THE NATURALIST

According to the ninety-first version of the fable, dawn arises without really dissipating the state of intoxication: McIntosh, unsure, seated on the armrest of a chair, hesitates between living and sinking even further; Percival, slightly less drunk, takes the opportunity to address his master with a very personal lullaby which resembles words of comfort: You observe me, you are human: interpretation is a bad habit, perhaps we've finally tracked down what is particular to men (it would be particularly human to look at other primates like an assistant-owner up and down with a measuring gaze; you will find what distinguishes man from animal precisely there, in the alarming desire to distinguish between man and animal). You look at me settled down at the typewriter: your calculations are correct, your eye is that of the naturalist, permanent and translucent; you spy and approve; you take notes of each of my gestures in a small notebook, and I take that exhaustiveness for a proof of love: except for you and my old wet nurse, who would worry about the number of meals I have a day? It is not that disagreeable to be the subject of your investigation, I'm telling you honestly, even if I look like I'm reduced to slavery – my part has its charms: to be a guinea pig is flattering, the profession of typist is noble, the Remington has very pleasing reflections, a harmonious and always docile mechanism, the bananas are the nectar from Olympus, albeit thicker, and combining the letters of the alphabet is somewhat exhilarating. Besides, you must know it, you are a human being after all, you have been dealing with the combinations of your spelling book for ever: to sit at the Remington would do you much good; it would convert a fatality attributed to your species (to express oneself, to always express oneself) in a board game. That's why I invite you to go back to it: if you want to discover large numbers and see how a primate adapts his intelligence to an abstract situation, the best thing would be to place your hands there where I had mine, on that keyboard, then to do scales instead of me.

I'll be right behind you: I will show you the same consideration, the same kindness (that I received from the very beginning); I will offer you board and lodging, I won't be mean with bananas, I will authorise you time for sleep and will even give you a party – I will be your lab assistant in order to finally give you the opportunity to assume, as the subject of an experiment, your animality: then and only then will you be able to access knowledge, and to understand finally what it means to be a primate, to struggle with a lexicon, show intelligence while looking for lice, tear oneself from the undergrowth of instinct, become aware of one's ape-self, a self more poetic than foreseen, and in the end access like an animal, refinement through mischief.

(Other versions of the fable (ninety-second and ninety-third) prolong over three chapters that scene of seduction between Percival the smooth talker, bewitching like Mephistopheles, skilful, suave, sometimes manipulative – and McIntosh, as a young and not so young scientist confused by the effect of the brandy, falling under the charm of his ape or at least of his ape's speech; one of those versions replaces the speech with a waltz.)

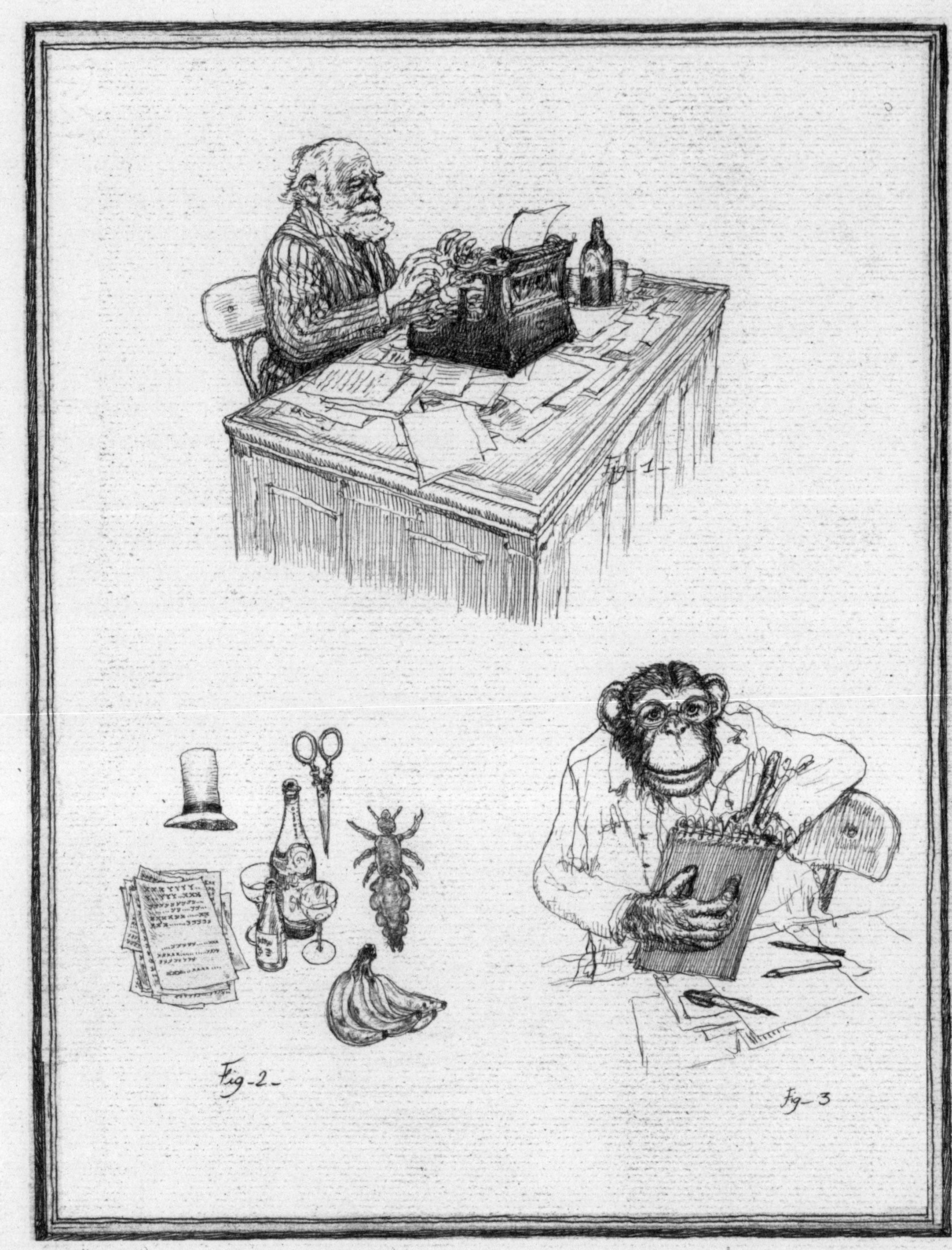
Fig-1-
Fig-2-
Fig-3

Chapter 59

THE ANIMAL
CHOOSES
A REPLACEMENT

The ninety-fourth version of the fable: above our heads, as from the very first days, the noise of a typewriter, that of each key and each rod (let's call it *hammer*) hitting the page through the ribbon (there must be something brutal in that precision of the letter that lodges exactly at the right spot, exactly at the right time): McIntosh is seated on his chair, grown old through weariness, the end of the day, the trials of the day before, all the alcohol mixed together, the combined intoxication of the tightrope walker and the boxing champion; one could see him with white hair on his shoulders, a receding hairline, a stoop and the look of a Darwin or a Leonardo da Vinci as he gazed contemplatively at his latest self-portrait. He is typing: his turn now to discover the combinations, the pleasure or boredom it implies; his turn to try his luck, to put his will aside and tap blindly on his keyboard to see if the gods of good luck and the dice with 26 sides give him the right to manage an acceptable line, at least one line, like *The little love-god lying once asleep*, and to be happy about it, to declare himself nevertheless responsible for this line (the desire to be an author, even though a miserable plagiarist, finally taking over the abnegation of the copyist) — *laid by his side his heart inflaming brand.* He types — during that time, Percival seated on the corner of a chair, fulfils his duty as observer: neutral and impartial lab assistant, in the style of the bailiff or the sphinx, the dignity of the scientist respecting his procedure to the point of wishing to disappear (and become again an abstraction among so many others).

He types, his white hair keeping up the pace: eternity will offer him a second-hand glory, the merit of skilfully writing without mistake *The*

Invisible Man or *The Lady of the Camellias*, one embedded in the other; eternity plus one week plus one day will surely give him the opportunity to compare himself to, then to think he is William Shakespeare and Christopher Marlowe, before mixing them up and identifying himself with both – both at the same time. While waiting to finish a thousand versions of *Twelfth Night*, all similar except for one letter, McIntosh accepts the part of copyist taking the place of the copyist, as one says simulacrum of simulacrum (and draft of draft), showing good will, almost repentance, inflicting on himself tortures imposed on others before him (the tortures of the keyboard): he forces himself to write *Percival's Adventures*, all the versions of the same fable, those we were given to read and those we are left to discover: two or three versions still, the last ones, having arrived late, written with leftover ink – in them we will discover a certain mellowness close to resignation, in other words, serenity, the sign of old age, approaching death, alleviated anxiety, universal reconciliation of the author, whoever he is, with the world and its countless twaddle.

Let's take a closer look, without saying a word (twilight, then pitch black, it's the hour when the goblins of the Brothers Grimm or Perrault, the elves, the demons and angels, the young mice, the scholarly cats, the sorceresses, move forward then retreat on tiptoes, accomplishing what had to be accomplished): the ornamental garden at midnight, the parks, the alleys, the recesses, the escheated pavilions, a laboratory set up with bits and pieces, a room almost bare, a seat, a typewriter and finally a typist. So focused is he on his writing that he doesn't see his chimpanzee climbing on a stool (the same stool that was successfully used by his ancestor Sultan to reach his bananas in 1925), opening a louvre window, going through the opening and disappearing for good, in other words *for ever*, after having cast on that crazy McIntosh (crazy and dishevelled), an indefinable last look – (indefinable? One wouldn't have any problem seeing in it compassion, curiosity, gratefulness, yes, and the most bestial friendship).

Chapter 60

THE ANIMAL
TAKES LEAVE

(In one of the last versions of the fable, not retained, Percival the chimpanzee takes leave of McIntosh the lab assistant: hug, play face and flee.)

THE ANIMAL LEAVES FOR GOOD

The ninety-fifth version gives the last portrait of Percival the ape (grown old, weary, filled with a hope similar to sleep), and puts in his mouth these parting words of farewell:

I am not Shakespeare, I don't leave behind me Sonnets and Dramas and the *Merry Wives*, I didn't invent Ophelia floating in her tattered rags, I didn't even invent her randomly, and if ever one finds after my death a scrap of Hamlet in my drawers, it won't be the legacy of my genius – it will be at most the proof of my capacity as imitator, capable as I am to imitate genius give or take a comma or two.

I have not succeeded in becoming Shakespeare, which would have been one way as any other to become human, but I am a living chimpanzee, I must take my destiny as ape lightly; with a bit of luck, all the eternity of writing for nothing will be followed by its eighth day of rest: then it will be the return to my fellow apes, meantime I wouldn't have aged one bit: the girls will be there, I shall lift armfuls of them, the wait won't have embittered them, they would have found ways to comfort themselves, it's a way to make oneself sublime, they would have forgotten me then they will remember, according to the cycle of the seasons; under the trees I will introduce myself to the young ladies of my childhood, I shall be haughty, just what's necessary, I shall have the halo of the poet who has overcome the sentence, a serpent with seven heads, a reputation will have preceded me in the forest, at the same time as the cry of other howler monkeys, from tree top to tree top; none will be fooled by that, but neither will they hate me for it. As soon as spring comes, I will regain the habits of my youth, and the following summer the fruits of each past summer; I will gradually forget the alphabet, only keeping the essential to brighten up the mating displays, or to say goodbye, or make promises; I shall forget the spells of the combination; I shall sometimes remember the Remington, but in the absence of a model, it will every day resemble a little bit more a bag filled with white speckled pebbles similar to quails' eggs; will remain also the face of my lab assistant, a gardener, a hundred year-old youth, at the same time young and old, easy-going and greedy for spectacular results. I shall have the opportunity, I hope, to bite into halves of mangoes, kiss first-degree female cousins to catch up with lost time, rock myself in the rainy season under the leaf of a banana tree, then hunt all day for sweet black ants with a reed. I shall have to count on those pages written for days on end — fables, fairy tales, pieces of formal logic — to give to all things the intensity it was perhaps lacking.

Chapter 61

THE ANIMAL
MAKES HIMSELF VANISH

Percival having done a runner, the ninety-sixth, ninety-seventh and ninety-eighth versions of the fable, all in unison, take word for word the scene of the escape: McIntosh remains alone, his silence is serene, not despairing, he would have avoided a heart-rending separation, he doesn't complain about the loss of a friend entirely contained in his drafts (the disappearance of the friend will be comforted by a thousand pages of writing celebrating the friend, portrait, slice of life, story, panegyric; with time, as solitary as he could become, McIntosh will find the opportunity to make through writing other candid hugs; he will find again the friendship itself made of embraces, real presence and absence).

Here are the epilogues as one recreates them — but reality, if it exists, could be different, could do without heart-rending goodbyes, louvre windows and full moon nights, eschewing Percival's escape as well as McIntosh's stupor: according to the last version of the fable, the very last, the ninety-ninth, the chimpanzee remains faithful to his lab assistant, his partner and only friend: instead of fleeing, he chooses to grow old next to his master, soothed by a routine, governed by the sound of a typewriter, fed a million bananas, taking advantage of a purely hypothetical immortality, or a suspension of time comparable to, let's say, a rainy Sunday afternoon: he stays there, renouncing wild life, convinced now to never return to the place he has come from.

Epilogue

(One has to add this still: to give his ape at least the illusion of escape, McIntosh writes seven or seven hundred pages on Percival's flight: it starts at night, through the same louvre window, under the full moon, is carried out over the roofs, eaves, gutters, stairs, fences, continues from street to street and town to town, crosses borders, pursues journeys, improvises adventures of stolen passages on freighters from Genoa to Djakarta while reviving from memory the exploits already narrated a thousand times of chimney sweepers gone to clear the Moluccas — still seven or seven hundred pages to say how Percival sets foot on his island again, recognises his country by its scents, finds his way without a compass by relying on the rising sun, returns to his forest, shakes the fern of his childhood, bites into fruits whose existence he has forgotten for years, holds his breath, listens attentively to the cries of his fellow apes, and with a bit of luck, falls into the arms of brothers and sisters who have been for ever waiting for him. He is not sure yet of the choice of each of his words, from *louvre window* to *brothers and sisters*, but McIntosh knows it in advance, or guesses it: the story of the flight of Percival the ape will reach its conclusion on the name of his island: Borneo.)

TABLE
OF THE ETHOGRAMS

GENERAL CLASSIFICATION OF THE ETHOGRAMS

Behaviours of approach and negotiation

Affiliative or sexual behaviours

Agnostic behaviours

cover: design Lili Fleury & drawings Nicolas de Crécy

with the support of Région Ile-de-France
&

with the support of ![cnap] Centre national des arts plastiques,
Ministère de la Culture et de la Communication (research grant)

&
for the translation with
the assistance of the Ministère français chargé de la culture - Centre national du livre